SEASONS OF WOMAN

Song, Poetry, Ritual, Prayer, Myth, Story

Penelope Washbourn

Published in San Francisco by
HARPER & ROW, PUBLISHERS
New York, Hagerstown, San Francisco, London

In memory of my mother

MARGARET LYALL WASHBOURN

1912–1979

FIRST EDITION
Designed by Donna Davis

Library of Congress Cataloging in Publication Data

Main entry under title:

Seasons of woman.

1. Women—Literary collections.   2. Folk literature.
3. Women (in religion, folklore, etc.)   I. Washbourn, Penelope.
PN6071.W7S4   1979   808.8'0352   78-20582

---

79 80 81 82 83 10 9 8 7 6 5 4 3 2 1

CONTENTS

Preface   xi

1.   Girl-Child: The Celebration of Youth   1

2.   Menstruation: The Passage to Maturity   13

3.   Separation from Home: The Wedding   29

4.   Married Life   37

5.   Passionate Woman   53

6.   Woman's Body: The Sexual Center   77

7.   Motherhood   113

8.   The Changing Seasons   135

Notes   164

List of Plates

Page 1   Apache tribe by A. F. Randall before 1884. Reproduced through the courtesy of Lowie Museum of Anthropology, University of California, Berkeley.

Page 7   Hooker Family Portraits. Reproduced through the courtesy of the Bancroft Library, University of California, Berkeley.

Page 9   Mexico, Yucatan, Chichen Itza by E. L. Crandall, 1925. Reproduced through the courtesy of Lowie Museum of Anthropology, University of California, Berkeley.

Page 13   Southwest U.S.A., "Nalta's Sister" by A. F. Randall before 1884. Reproduced through the courtesy of Lowie Museum of Anthropology, University of California, Berkeley.

Page 20   Philippines by Roy F. Barton pre-1918. Reproduced through the courtesy of Lowie Museum of Anthropology, University of California, Berkeley.

Page 25   Reproduced through the courtesy of Megan McKenna.

Page 29   California, Regua, Yurok tribe by A. L. Kroeber 1907. "Alice Frank." Reproduced through the courtesy of Lowie Museum of Anthropology, University of California, Berkeley.

Page 33   Hooker Family Portraits. Reproduced through the courtesy of the Bancroft Library, University of California, Berkeley.

Page 37   Philippines by Roy F. Barton pre-1918, Kalinga man and woman. Reproduced through the courtesy of Lowie Museum of Anthropology, University of California, Berkeley.

Page 39   Reproduced through the courtesy of Megan McKenna.

Page 47   Hooker Family Portraits. Reproduced through the courtesy of the Bancroft Library, University of California, Berkeley.

Page 53   Reproduced through the courtesy of Megan McKenna.

Page 64   Reproduced through the courtesy of Megan McKenna.

Page 74   Philippines, Ifugao by Roy F. Barton pre-1918. Reproduced through the courtesy of Lowie Museum of Anthropology, University of California, Berkeley.

Page 77   Reproduced through the courtesy of Katy Raddatz and the *San Francisco Examiner.*

Page 113   Africa, Uganda, Madi Tribe. Reproduced through the courtesy of Lowie Museum of Anthropology, University of California, Berkeley.

Page 120   California, Ukiah Valley, Pomo Tribe by S. A. Barrett 1904. Reproduced through the courtesy of Lowie Museum of Anthropology, University of California, Berkeley.

Page 125   Reproduced through the courtesy of Katy Raddatz and the *San Francisco Examiner.*

Page 131   Reproduced through the courtesy of Megan McKenna.

Page 135   Philippines, Benguet, by Roy F. Barton pre-1918. Igorot Woman. Reproduced through the courtesy of Lowie Museum of Anthropology, University of California, Berkeley.

Page 143   Hooker Family Portraits. Reproduced through the courtesy of the Bancroft Library, University of California, Berkeley.

Page 155   Reproduced through the courtesy of Megan McKenna.

Jacket plates: Photos 1, 8 and 15 are courtesy of Megan McKenna. All other photos are courtesy of Lowie Museum of Anthropology, University of California, Berkeley.

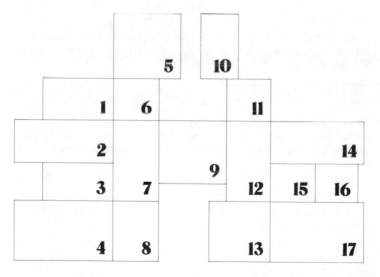

Acknowledgments

"To the Anxious Mother" by Valente Malangatana, trans. Dorothy Guedes and Philippa Rumsey, from *Poems from Black Africa*, edited by Langston Hughes. 1963. Reprinted by permission of Indiana University Press.

"Poem 50," *Poems of the Kaleva District*, Elias Lönnrot, comp., Francis P. Magoun, Jr., trans., Cambridge, Mass.: Harvard University Press, Copyright © 1963 by the President and Fellows of Harvard College.

"Poem 25," from *The Old Kalevala and Certain Antecedents*, Elias Lönnrot, comp., Francis P. Magoun, Jr., trans., Cambridge, Mass.: Harvard University Press, Copyright © 1969 by the President and Fellows of Harvard College.

Blessingway, by permission, Leland C. Wyman, Tucson: University of Arizona Press, copyright 1970.

"After Grief" from *Collected Poems: The Two Seasons* by Dorothy Livesay. Copyright © Dorothy Livesay, 1972. Reprinted by permission of McGraw-Hill Ryerson Limited.

"Love Song," from *The Glory of Egypt* by M. Samivel by permission of the publisher, Vanguard Press, Inc. All rights reserved, 1955.

"Childlessness," poem by G. R. D. Maclean in *Poems of the Western Highlanders* (1961) is reproduced by permission of SPCK.

"A Faithful Wife" by Chang Chi; Kenneth Rexroth, *100 More Poems from the Chinese. Love and the Turning Year.* Copyright © 1970 by Kenneth Rexroth. Reprinted by permission of New Directions.

"Married Love," "The warm rain falls unfeeling . . .," "A Song of White Hair," "You held my lotus blossom," Numbers I, II, and III, "If You don't know how . . .," "Spring Song," "The hardest thing in the world . . .," "O Flowery Mountain Slopes," and "On your slender body . . ." from *The Orchid Boat: Women Poets of China*, edited and translated by Kenneth Rexroth and Ling Chung, 1972. Reprinted by permission of The Seabury Press.

"With Child" from *Travelling Standing Still* by Genevieve Taggard, 1928. Reprinted by permission of Marcia D. Liles, estate of Genevieve Taggard.

From *Sumerian Mythology* by Samuel Noah Kramer, 1961, by permission of the American Philosophical Society, Pennsylvania.

"This is the truth my lover," "Washing and pounding of clothes," "Parting of a newly-wedded couple" from *Ancient Poetry from China, Japan and India*, trans. Henry W. Wells. Reprinted by permission of the University of South Carolina Press.

"A woman to her lover," "Waiting for Mother," "Lullaby" from *African*

PREFACE

The idea for any book arises from a particular situation.
Each book has a story. In this case the story behind the
compilation of this collection is simple. As I was
writing my first book, *Becoming Woman* (1977), I
began to read North American Indian prayers of
dedication for the young girl as she started out on her
life's journey. What impressed and surprised me, a
modern Western woman, was their sense of reverence
for the goodness and beauty of the woman's life. I
realized that I, as one raised in a Christian religious and
cultural context, had never been taught to celebrate the
many stages of my female identity in the context of
the religious community.

This book is a collection of many different types of
literature: songs, folksongs, prayers, liturgies, poems,
prose. The book aims to provide the reader with a
sense of how women express their own spiritual
sensibilities about their identities as women. I have
looked for words said and sung by women, words
written by women, words prayed by women. Even in
societies where men play the dominant role in culture
and religion, women play a major part in those
ceremonies *specifically* to do with women's events.

Too often, what women sang and celebrated in their
own secret ceremonies has been lost forever. Sometimes, early researchers were not interested in the
prayers surrounding the birth of a child; sometimes
they were excluded (by virtue of being men) from the

observation of women's ceremonies. For pre-Christian rites that surround the worship of the fertility principle, the later Christian reporters of such ceremonies were biased and disapproving and relied on gossip. Too often in my search have I come to a dead end and wondered what has been lost.

Most of the selections come from cultures where anthropologists began research in the late nineteenth century and recorded the songs and prayers. Many are from cultures whose traditional patterns of life are still intact and whose women continue to sing such songs. Some of the selections are from myth and folklore, others from European and North American poets.

I have not separated "religious" from "nonreligious" materials. The tradition of female spirituality is embodied in the experience of a woman's life in its many changes. Too often the term 'spirituality' has referred to something 'other-worldly' or godly; in the songs in this collection, the spiritual and the ordinary are intertwined. Woman's religious events (among others) are those that concern her own bodily experience as woman; the symbols and forms for worship, prayer and celebration are drawn from her whole life.

I have included the writings of some modern women poets to indicate the continuity between the primitive or ancient traditions and those of modern women writers. The spiritual tradition of women in our own times has been carried on more by the artists and writers than in the official context of religion. This situation is beginning to change as women play an increasing role in traditional religions and create new forms of religious expression.

The selections in the book reflect the primary experience of woman in the precontemporary age: a life centered around the experience of female

sexuality in its fertile aspect. As modern readers we
may feel a lack of alternative perspectives and roles
for the woman's life and perhaps a lack of sympathy
for the agonies of barrenness, for example, in the
women of other cultures. The selections are not
intended to be prescriptive or exhaustive. They reflect
rather the range of feelings and situations experienced
by women of many cultures and ages, and in many
cases the modern reader can identify with certain
aspects of the selections. The centrality of a woman's
fertility is an aspect the modern reader will notice;
it was the cause of much joy and pain and was
experienced as connecting woman with the forces of
life itself. It is this sense of the holy power in their own
bodies that engenders reverence, thankfulness, and
even awe and fear and that often distinguishes the
women of traditional societies from contemporary
women raised in a technological society. The question
for modern readers, both women and men, is not how
they can duplicate the past but how they can discover
in their many and varied lifestyles and new roles a
sense of worship in the many seasons of life.

The research for this work was partially financed
by the University of Manitoba and by a leave fellow-
ship from the Canada Council. I am immensely
indebted to my research assistant of two years, Gaile
Whelan Enns, whose energy and enthusiasm for the
project contributed greatly to its execution.

I am thankful to all those who support me in my life
and work, my husband and family, my friends, my
students and colleagues and the many scholars who are
interested in the reevaluation of woman's role in
religion. I thank also my editor, Marie Cantlon, who
has been, as before, faithful in her encouragement,
patient in her persistence and wise in her judgment.

THE BLESSING OF WOMAN

The Invocation of the Graces

I bathe thy palms
In showers of wine,
In the lustral fire,
In the seven elements,
In the juice of the rasps,
In the milk of honey,
And I place the nine pure choice graces
In thy fair fond face,
> The grace of form,
> The grace of voice,
> The grace of fortune,
> The grace of goodness,
> The grace of wisdom,
> The grace of charity,
> The grace of choice maidenliness,
> The grace of whole-souled loveliness,
> The grace of goodly speech.

Dark is yonder town,
Dark are those therein,
Thou art the brown swan,
Going in among them.
Their hearts are under thy control,
Their tongues are beneath thy sole,
Nor will they ever utter a word
> To give thee offence.

A shade art thou in the heat,
A shelter art thou in the cold,
Eyes art thou to the blind,
A staff art thou to the pilgrim,
An island art thou at sea,
A fortress art thou on land,

A well art thou in the desert,
   Health art thou to the ailing.

Thine is the skill of the Fairy Woman,
Thine is the virtue of Bride the calm,
Thine is the faith of Mary the mild,
Thine is the tact of the woman of Greece,
Thine is the beauty of Emir the lovely,
Thine is the tenderness of Darthula delightful,
Thine is the courage of Maebh the strong,
   Thine is the charm of Binne-bheul.

Thou art the joy of all joyous things,
Thou art the light of the beam of the sun,
Thou art the door of the chief of hospitality,
Thou art the surpassing star of guidance,
Thou art the step of the deer of the hill,
Thou art the step of the steed of the plain,
Thou art the grace of the swan of swimming,
      Thou art the loveliness of all lovely desires.

The lovely likeness of the Lord
Is in thy pure face,
The loveliest likeness that
Was upon earth.

The best hour of the day be thine,
The best day of the week be thine,
The best week of the year be thine,
The best year in the Son of God's domain be thine.

Peter has come and Paul has come,
James has come and John has come,
Muriel and Mary Virgin have come,
Uriel the all-beneficient has come,
Ariel the beauteousness of the young has come,
Gabriel the seer of the Virgin has come,

Raphael the prince of the valiant has come,
And Michael the chief of the hosts has come,
  And Jesus Christ the mild has come,
  And the Spirit of true guidance has come,
  And the King of kings has come on the helm,
  To bestow on thee their affection and their love,
    To bestow on thee their affection and their love.

A Gaelic blessing for the young girl*

Chapter
One

Girl-Child:
The Celebration
of Youth

BEING BORN

She was unloaded and delivered to us, glory be!
Unloaded from her mother, the little one, delivered,
And we all say Glory Be!

An Eskimo birth song[1]

TO THE ANXIOUS MOTHER

Into your arms I came
when you bore me, very anxious
you, who were so alarmed
at that monstrous moment
fearing that God might take me.
Everyone watched in silence
to see if the birth was going well
everyone washed their hands
to be able to receive the one who came from Heaven
and all the women were still and afraid.
But when I emerged
from the place where you sheltered me so long
at once I drew my first breath
at once you cried out with joy
the first kiss was my grandmother's.
And she took me at once to the place
where they kept me, hidden away
everyone was forbidden to enter my room
because everyone smelt bad
and I all fresh, fresh
breathed gently, wrapped in my napkins.
But grandmother, who seemed like a madwoman,
always looking and looking again
because the flies came at me

and the mosquitoes harried me.
God who also watched over me
was my old granny's friend.

A modern poem from Mozambique[2]

It is that, when she has given birth to a child, as soon
as its father finds out that it is a girl, then the man
asks the midwife, another woman, to wrap up the child
in a warm blanket. Then the man takes eagle down and
takes the child in his arms and goes inland. When he
reaches a patch of salal berry bushes he takes the down
and breaks it up. Then he puts the down over the salal
leaves, while he is still carrying the child in his arms.
When he has done so he prays to the down and to the
salal bushes and says, "Go on, Supernatural Ones,
please, look at me and my child which I got by good
luck and please, give over your power of success to her
and your (power of) containing wealth to her that she
may be rich in every way like you, Supernatural Ones;
and also, protect her that she may not have bad luck in
her work when she is grown up, and also that she may
be a real dancer, Supernatural One, please," says he
and he goes home to his house. For four days he is
doing so to his daughter. Then he stops.

*The treatment of a girl who is
to be a dancer in the Kwakiutl Indians*[3]

Sophie's kitchen was crammed with excited women. They had come to see Sophie's brand-new twins. Sophie was on a mattress beside the cook stove. The twin girls were in small basket papoose cradles, woven by Sophie herself. The babies were wrapped in cotton wool which made their dark little faces look darker; they were laced into their baskets and stuck up at the edge of Sophie's mattress beside the kitchen stove. Their brown winkled faces were like potatoes baked in their jackets, their hands no bigger than brown spiders.

They were thrilling, those very very tiny babies. Everybody was excited over them. I sat down on the floor close to Sophie.

"Sophie, if the baby was a girl it was to have my name. There are two babies and I have only one name. What are we going to do about it?"

"The biggest and the best is yours," said Sophie.

My Em'ly lived three months. Sophie's Maria lived three weeks. I bought Em'ly's tombstone. Sophie bought Maria's.

The birth of twins to a Canadian
West Coast Indian woman[4]

When a girl is born by her mother, she is washed by the midwife who takes care of the woman who has given birth. After she has washed her, she wraps her in warm covers. Now the mother of the child takes a little mountain goat wool and she takes a narrow strip of cotton cloth. She takes a little wool and puts it on the narrow strip of cotton cloth. Then she prays to it and says, "Now great supernatural power of the

Supernatural-One-of-the-Rocks, look at what I am
doing to you, for I pray you that you, please, have
mercy on my child and that you give her success in
picking all kinds of berries on the mountain; and this,
that she may have success in obtaining property and
be rich like you, great Supernatural One; and this,
that you protect her that nothing evil may happen to
her when she goes up (the mountain) picking berries
on the mountain; and this, (against) sickness. Go on,
please, listen to my prayer to you, supernatural power
of the Supernatural-One-of-the-Rocks," says she.

As soon as she stops praying she wraps the narrow
strip of cotton cloth around the four strings of wool.
She puts them into a small basket in which the clothes
of her child are. Now she waits for the navel cord of
her child to come off. As soon as it is off she ties it
around the right hand of her child. Now it stays on
her hand, and until the time when the child is nine
months old it will not be taken off. As soon as the
child is nine months old her mother takes the remains
of the wool and she takes the four strings and wraps
around them the cotton cloth that has been washed,
around the four strings of wool. Then she ties it
around the right hand of her child and she also takes
one piece of wool and cuts it up so that it is like flour.
She puts a little water with it so that it becomes
pastry. Then she prays to the finely cut wool and says,
"O, supernatural power of the Supernatural-One-of-
the-Rocks, go on, look at what I am doing to you, for
I pray you to take mercy on my child and please, let
her be successful in getting property and let nothing
evil happen to her when she goes up the mountain
picking all kinds of berries; and please, protect her,
Supernatural One," says she as she puts her first
finger into what is like milk, the wool mixed with
water, and she puts it on the tongue of the child. Four

times she does so. When she has finished she suckles her child. Now for four days she does this in the morning, then she stops after this.

Now this woman who has been treated grows up and she really gets much when she picks all kinds of berries on the berry picking places on the mountains of Knights Inlet and therefore she has many berry cakes and crabapples and Viburnum. She is rich in property, for the woman is industrious. That is the end.

The treatment of a first-born girl among the Kwakiutl Indians[5]

At half past three, everything slumbered still in a primal blue, blurred and dewy, and as I went down the sandy road the mist, grounded by its own weight, bathed first my legs, then my well-built little body, reaching at last to my mouth and ears, and finally to that most sensitive part of all, my nostrils. I went alone, for there were no dangers in that freethinking countryside. It was on that road and at that hour that I first became aware of my own self, experienced an inexpressible state of grace, and felt one with the first breath of air that stirred, the first bird, and the sun so newly born that it still looked not quite round.

"Beauty," my mother would call me, and "Jewel of pure gold"; then she would let me go, watching her creation—her masterpiece, as she said—grow smaller as I ran down the slope. I may have been pretty; my mother and the pictures of me at that period do not always agree. But what made me pretty at that moment was my youth and the dawn, my blue eyes deepened

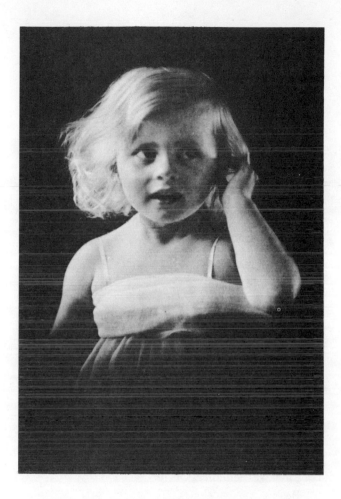

by all the greenery all around me, my fair locks that
would only be brushed smooth on my return, and my
pride at being awake when other children were asleep.

From Colette's autobiography[6]

BOYS AND GIRLS

Boys and girls come out to play
In air, in water;
All together duck, dive, somersault,
Push the waves about as if they owned
A cool blue liquid fortune;

Then, mysteriously,
For no one gives a signal,
They climb the ladder, throw
Their spongy selves on silver dock,
The pale boards darken round their bodies
Where the water runs.

The plumpness on the girls is new
And not yet of them;
Awkwardly as the farmer's boy
His Sunday suit
They wear a flounce of hips,
The prickling breasts,
Their minds have gone away to sleep
In a far country;
Nothing is, except to tease
And nurse them into women,
They do not speak to boys unless to jeer,
And sit apart,
But out of the corners of their eyes
They look at them incessantly.

Boys are proud, groin
A phoenix, fire and ash
And new-found agony;
Minds are here, not stars away
And fine nerves sing
Like wire stretched from pole to pole
In a prairie wind;

Nowhere are they cradled
In a warmth of fat
So they must tremble, boast,
Insult the lolling maidens,
Girls they hate
Whose bodies swim in their veins,
Whom somehow they must touch.

Mysteriously, again,
For no one gives a signal,
It's water time.
Pink girls rise and run, sticky
As from candy at a fair,
Shriek and mimic fear
When the crowing boys push
Into the quivering lake
The girls they'll kiss next year.

By the modern Canadian poet Anne Wilkinson[7]

Alalai Evohe!
Here's to our girls
    With their tangling curls,
        Legs a-wiggle,
        Bellies a-jiggle,
            A riot of hair,
        A fury of feet,
Evohe! Evohai! Evohe!
                        as they pass
    Dancing,
            dancing,
                    dancing,
                        to greet
Athene of the House of Brass!

The chorus of the Spartans singing
in Lysistrata, *by Aristophanes*[8]

Aj-ja-japa-pe.
Bring out your hair-ornaments!
We're only girls
rejoicing with each other!
Aj-ja-japape.

Difficult times,
shortages of meat
have smitten everyone:
stomachs hollow,
meat-trays empty.
Aj-ja-japape.

Can you see out there?
The men are coming home,
dragging seals
towards our village!
Aj-ja-japape.

Joy has distorted
everything in sight:
the leather boats lift themselves
away from their ropes,
the straps follow them,
the earth itself
floats freely in the air!
Aj-ja-japape.

Plenty visits us again:
times when feasts
bind us together.
Aj-ja-japape.

Do you recognize
the smell of boiling pots,
and blubber squelching
in the corner of the bench?
Aj-ja-japape, hu-hue!
Joyfully we welcome
those who bring us wealth!

An Eskimo song[9]

When they are just beginning to talk about the ceremony, the girl goes to the woman who is going to take care of her. She brings an eagle feather to this woman. The girls holds the butt end and motions four times with the tip end of the feather toward the woman. The woman takes it the fourth time. Then the woman will take care of the girl. She will rub her and push her out to run.

Right from this time the girl calls that woman "mother," even though she is no relative, and this woman calls the girl "my daughter." And they give each other presents throughout life.

An Apache ceremony at a girl's maturation[10]

This is the truth, my lover:
My childhood could not last;
Since my long hair was clipped
Full eight long years have passed.
Blooming like a fruit tree,
I am a secret stream
Running beneath earth's surface
And you my constant dream.
    I, too, have prayed the gods
    To make my childhood stay,
    But time must take its course
    And love will have its way.

An ancient poem from Japan[11]

Chapter
Two

Menstruation:
The Passage
to Maturity

heye neye yana
Now she is dressing up her child,
Now she is dressing up her child,
Now she is dressing up her child, holaghei.
Now the child of White Shell Woman,
    now she is dressing her up,
In the center of the White Shell house,
    now she is dressing her up,
On the even white shell floor covering,
    now she is dressing her up,
On the smooth floor covering of soft fabrics,
    now she is dressing her up.
White Shell Girl, now she is dressing her up,
Her white shell shoes, now she is dressing her up,
Her white shell leggings, now she is dressing her up,
Her white shell clothes, now she is dressing her up,
Now, a perfect white shell having been placed on her
    forehead,
        now she is dressing her up,
Her white shell head plume, now she is dressing her up,
Now at its tip there are small blue male birds, truly
    beautiful;
        it is shining at its tip,
        now she is dressing her up,
They call as they are playing; their voices are beautiful;
        now she is dressing her up,
She is decorated with soft fabrics,
        now she is dressing her up,
She is decorated with jewels,
        now she is dressing her up.
Before her, it is blessed; now she is dressing her up,
Behind her, it is blessed; now she is dressing her up,
Now with long life and everlasting beauty,
        now she is dressing her up.

Now she is dressing up her child,
Now she is dressing up her child, it is said.

*Part of the Navaho Blessing Way ceremonies
for ushering the pubescent girl into society to
invoke positive blessing on her*[12]

We think of a woman's life as blocked out in parts.
One is girlhood, one is young womanhood, one is
middle age, and one is old age. The songs are supposed
to carry her through them. The first songs describe
the holy home and the ceremony. Later come the
songs about the flowers and the growing things. These
stand for her youth, and as the songs go through the
seasons the girl is growing up and reaching old age.

This song is about flowers. We are taking this girl
through a beautiful life. This is the conception of a
beautiful life for the Apache. We take the girl through
beautiful lands, past flowers, through seasons with
their fruits. The translation doesn't mean much, but
there is a great deal to it if you think about it.

*An Apache perspective on the songs
for the girl's initiation*[13]

SLOW BUFFALO'S PRAYER

"O You, White Swan Power of the place where we always face, who control the path of the generations and of all that moves, we are about to purify a virgin, that her generations to come may walk in a sacred manner upon that path which You control. There is a place for You in the pipe! Help us with Your two red and blue days!"

The Power of the south was then put in the pipe, and, holding now a pinch of tobacco up to the heavens, Slow Buffalo continued. "O Wakan-Tanka, Grandfather, behold us! We are about to offer the pipe to You!" [Then holding the tobacco to the earth]:

"O You, Grandmother, upon whom the generations of the people have walked, may White Buffalo Cow Woman Appears and her generations walk upon you in a sacred manner in the winters to come. O Mother Earth, who gives forth fruit, and who is as a mother to the generations, this young virgin who is here today will be purified and made sacred; may she be like You, and may her children and her children's children walk the sacred path in a holy manner. Help us, O Grandmother and Mother, with Your red and blue days!"

The Earth, as Grandmother and Mother, was now in the tobacco, and was placed in the pipe, and again Slow Buffalo held tobacco towards the heavens and prayed.

"O Wakan-Tanka, behold us! We are about to offer this pipe to You." [Then pointing the same tobacco to the buffalo skull]: "O you, our four-legged relative, and who of all the four-legged peoples are nearest to the two-leggeds, you too are to be placed in the pipe, for you have taught us how you cleanse your young, and it is this way that we shall use in purifying White Buffalo Cow Woman Appears. I give to you as an offering, O four-legged, water, paint, cherry juice, and also grass. There is a place for you in the pipe— help us!"

Thus all the four-legged buffalo people were placed in the pipe, and now for the last time Slow Buffalo held tobacco up to Wakan-Tanka and prayed.

"O Wakan-Tanka and all the winged Powers of the universe, behold us! This tobacco I offer especially to You, the Chief of all the Powers, who is represented by the Spotted Eagle who lives in the depths of the heavens, and who guards all that is there! We are about to purify a young girl, who is soon to be a woman. May You guard those generations which will come forth from her! There is a place for You in the pipe— help us with the red and blue days!"

Preparing for womanhood among the Ogalala Sioux[14]

1.

I come to White Painted Woman,
By means of long life I come to her.
I come to her by means of her blessing,
I come to her by means of her good fortune,
I come to her by means of all her different fruits.
By means of the long life she bestows, I come to her.
By means of this holy truth she goes about.

2.

I am about to sing this song of yours,
    The song of long life.
Sun, I stand here on the earth with your song.
Moon, I have come in with your song.

3.

White Painted Woman's power emerges,
Her power for sleep.
White Painted Woman carries this girl;
She carries her through long life,
She carries her to good fortune,
She carries her to old age,
She bears her to peaceful sleep.

4.

You have started out on the good earth;
You have started out with good moccasins;
With moccasin strings of the rainbow, you have
    started out.
With moccasin strings of the sun rays, you have
    started out.
In the midst of plenty you have started out.

*Songs of maturation sung during girls'
puberty rites, from the Chiricahua*[15]

A girl for whom it is the very first time—she still not being united with a man so that children will be born—the very first time that the blood flows through her she tells about it:

"Blood has indeed flowed through me," she says as she tells about it. "Now it is all right! You say that you have become menstruant!" In this way, when she tells about it, she at once comes to be called Menstruating for the First Time. All right! Now it is this way: at once she is decorated. She is decorated with beads, she is decorated with bracelets. A tanned skin is inquired about, the skin of a deer which has not been killed with a gun, the skin of one which has not been killed with an arrow. That is called One Which Is Not Arrow-marked. That is what they inquire of each other about. "Where is there One Which Is Not Arrow-marked?" Even if it is small, even if it is narrow, it is obtained.

Menstruation ceremonies among the Navaho[16]

Dark young pine, at the center of the earth
    originating,
I have made your sacrifice.
Whiteshell, turquoise, abalone beautiful,
Jet beautiful, fool's gold beautiful, blue pollen beautiful,
    reed pollen, pollen beautiful, your sacrifice I have
    made.
This day your child I have become, I say.

Watch over me.
Hold your hand before me in protection.
Stand guard for me, speak in defense of me.
As I speak for you, so do ye.
As you speak for me, thus shall I do.
　　May it be beautiful before me.
　　May it be beautiful behind me,
　　May it be beautiful below me,
　　May it be beautiful above me,
　　May it be beautiful around me.

I am restored in beauty,
I am restored in beauty,
I am restored in beauty,
I am restored in beauty.

*The dedication of the father with daughters
during the puberty ceremony*[17]

And then I was thirteen years old. "Now is the time
when you must watch yourself; at last you are nearly
a young woman. Do not forget this which I tell you.
You might ruin your brothers if you are not careful.
The state of being a young woman is evil. The
manitous hate it. If any one is blessed by a manitou, if
he eats with a young woman he is then hated by the
one who blessed him and the (manitou) ceases to think
of him. That is why it is told us, 'be careful' and why
we are told about it beforehand. At the time when you
are a young woman, whenever you become a young
woman, you are to hide yourself. Do not come into
your wickiup. That is what you are to do." She
frightened me when she told me.

Lo, sure enough when I was thirteen and a half years
old, I was told, "Go get some wood and carry it on
your back." It was nearly noon when I started out.
When I was walking along somewhere, I noticed
something strange about myself. I was terribly
frightened at being in that condition. I did not know
how I became that way. "This must be the thing about
which I was cautioned when I was told," I thought.

I went and laid down in the middle of the thick forest
there. I was crying, as I was frightened. It was almost

the middle of summer after we had done our hoeing. After a while my mother got tired of waiting for me. She came to seek me. Soon she found me. I was then crying hard.

"Come, stop crying. It's just the way with us women. We have been made to be that way. Nothing will happen to you. You will have gotten over this now in the warm weather. Had it happened to you in winter you would have had a hard time. You would be cold when you bathed as you would have to jump into the water four times. That is the way it is when we first have it. Now, today, as it is warm weather, you may swim as slowly as you like when you swim," I was told. "Lie covered up. Do not try to look around. I shall go and make (a wickiup) for you," I was told.

From the autobiography of a Fox Indian Woman[18]

Now, while we dance
Come here to us
gentle Gaiety,
Revelry, Radiance

and you, Muses
with lovely hair

By the Greek poet Sappho[19]

THE GOOD-LOOKING BOY

The good-looking boy
Is waiting for me in the lane.
Why should I not go with him?

The fair-looking boy
Is waiting for me in the hall.
Why should I not go with him?

In my embroidered coat, my cloak of lain,
In my embroidered skirt, my gown of lain,
My dear, my darling,
Take me in your coach!

In my embroidered skirt, my gown of lain,
In my embroidered coat, my cloak of lain,
My dear, my darling,
Take me with you when you go home!

An ancient Chinese poem
from The Book of Songs[20]

THE DISTAFF

You leaped from the white horses
And raced madly into the deep wave—
But "I've got you, dear!" I shouted loudly.
And when you were the Tortoise
You ran skipping through the yard of the great court.
These are the things that I lament and
Sorrow over, my sad Baucis—these are

Little trails through my heart that are
Still warm—my remembrances of you.
For our former delights are ashes now.
When we were young girls we sat in our rooms
Without a care, holding our dolls and pretending
We were young brides. Remember—at dawn
The "mother," who distributed the wool
To the attendant servants, came and called
You to help with the salting of the meat.
And how afraid we were, when we were small.
Of Mormo—she had huge ears on her head.
Walked about on four feet,
And was always changing faces.
But when you mounted your husband's bed
You forgot all about those things.
All you heard from your mother
When you were still a little child.
Dear Baucis, Aphrodite set forgetfulness
In your heart.
And so I lament you and neglect my duties.
For I am not so irreverent as to set foot out-of-doors
Or to look upon a corpse with my eyes
Or let my hair loose in lamentation—
But a blush of grief tears my [cheeks].

By the Greek poet Erinna[21]

I searched,
I looked, but did not find.
Accompany me to Namutoni
and come back again.

Go ahead, I shall run
and shall meet you there,
Although I should bear ten children
the youngest is oshilumbu's child.
It's not possible to stitch up
youth, it is not a basket,
it's not possible to return into it
as people return into a realm.
We travel
by daddy Leo's ox-wagon
Don't say that it's a night that
I fear.

I come, because I'm forced to come.
My boy-friend travels
by bus
he is going to Munue gwa Ntinda.

Many thoughts and
contemplations trouble me.
When the moon is full like
day
I shall go to my friend.

I have young girls
I comfort Nepaka's baby
in a carrying bag of leopard skin,
if you girl only would hurry to
Ondambo,
come, let's mourn

let's cry for the death of the
heart, and for the pain of the
swollen breasts.

African initiation songs[22]

Men, divide into two groups oo
You whisper in my ear that I should go to you
what do you want from me
what do you want from me
don't look at me
or else they'll watch and hurt you the shark's teeth
what do you want from me

what do you want
today come close
I'll go with you
roll up your skirts roll up your skirts sky high
come see come see come see

Two Ebos play together
one Ebo is strong but the other is weak
(Dance)
We skirt the island and sing
we're going to the dance
(we want to go to the place of the dance)
because everybody has to come and watch the spectacle
we want to go to the place of the dance, come here
we skirt the island and sing
we utter here we utter there cries of joy
We can't contain our pleasure any longer
put the ornaments around our members
slowly slowly
and we are busy with our burden
to advance a little a little
We are standing on one leg we the young girls all
    together on the shore
we the young girls all together on the shore oo
stretch today stretch today may some of you
carry everything into the young girl's house
but nobody may touch may touch her private parts.

The dance of the women during
girls' puberty ceremonies[23]

Give me my little hoe
I go to the gardens.
The little gardens of the ground-nuts.

Give me my little hoe,
So that I can make ready the hymen.
You have seen your husband.

A hoeing song in preparation for marriage,
from the Chisungu[24]

She is graceful
My young darling
It is delight
To look at her
She has a bindiya worth ten rupees
Her hawal is seven eight
The chains are five rupees
The chains kiss her cheeks
What delight it is to see her!

An Indian folksong from the Maikal
Hills praising the child bride[25]

Chapter
Three

Separation from Home:
The Wedding

Clanged the keys on the table;
   Outside the horses neighed.
"O my mother, my dear mother!"
Cried the little maid.

" 'Tis all over, all over!
   No more am I free.
So sad is it to be married!"
   and she wept bitterly.

   "Send you your dear daughter
   Far away?" mourned she.
"But I follow, my husband,
   Lo, I follow thee!

"The man whom I wed now
   A stranger is he.
Yet knoweth my father
   To whom he gives me!"

A Ukrainian folksong[26]

BRIDESMAIDS' CAROL

First
Voice   Virginity O my virginity!
   Where will you go when I lose you?

Second
Voice   I'm off to a place I shall never come
       back from
   Dear Bride!
     I shall never come back to you
   Never!

By Sappho[27]

The sky is covered with darkness,
The tilting clouds begin to part,
The leaning bud-shaped clouds in the sky.
The lightning flashes here and there,
The thunder reverberates, rumbles and roars,
Sending echoes repeatedly to Ku-haili-moe,
To Ha'iha'i-lau-ahea,
To the women in the rising flames.
There was a seeking of the lost, now it is found—
A mate is found,
One to share the chills of winter.
The sky is changing,
For Hakoi-lani, the house of welcome where rest is found.
Love has made a plea
That you two become united.
Here is a perch, a heavenly resting place,
A perch, a perch in heaven.
There is a trembling, a rumbling, a crackling
A rattling above, a rattling below,
A rustling of the rolling pebbles of Ikuwa.
There are sounds of voices in an inhabited house,
But what voices are heard in any empty one?
You two are now one,
The darkness has begun to depart,
The east is beginning to brighten
For day is here at last!
The night has been made kapu
Until the light of day arrives.
You are wedded! Free [to each other],
The prayer of the priest has taken flight.
Day is here!
Amama, the kapu is freed!
It has flown to the darkness! flown to the waters!
The prayer has gone its way.

An ancient marriage chant from Hawaii[28]

Stop, father, stop! Do not fear me. Stop, my kind
sun. Do not be alarmed at me. I do not desire thy
house. I will not send thee on my business. Give me
thy good blessing now that I am going among strange
people. Bless me at a strange father's and mother's
house. Just look, dear father, towards the open field;
behold the kind sun through the window. On the open
field grows a lovely birch, in the sky shines the kind
sun, variegated leaves are fluttering in the wind, by
wind and storm they are blown down to the ground.
Stop, father, stop! Look not at the kind sun, gaze not
at the lovely sun. The real sun shines not, a real white
barked birch is not growing. Thy child stands before
thee. Variegated leaves are not fluttering in the wind,
are not shaken to the ground by violent gusts. Hot
tears are falling from the face of thy child. Stop,
father, stop! Fear me not, my kind father, be not
alarmed, my darling father. For thy bread, thy salt,
thy food, thy teaching, I fall down at thy dear feet, I
kiss thy precious hand. I do not mind spoiling my gala-
dress. I sink down at thy feet. Give me thy blessing.
I keep kissing thy hands, I do not spare myself. Bless
me, my father, to live with a stranger, to do the work
of a stranger.

Marriage customs of the Morduins [29]

I'm "wife"—I've finished that—
That other state—

I'm Czar—I'm "Woman" now—
It's safer so—

How odd the Girl's life looks
Behind this soft Eclipse—
I think that Earth feels so
To folks in Heaven—now—

This being comfort—then
That other kind—was pain—
But why compare?
I'm "Wife"! Stop there!

By Emily Dickinson, c.1860[30]

| The Bride: | Why hast thou left me? Whither fled, |
| | O maidenhead, O maidenhead? |

| Her Virginity: | Ah, never more, O maiden mine, |
| | Shall I be thine, shall I be thine! |

A bridal morning welcome by Sappho[31]

LAMENT FOR A MAIDENHEAD

First
Voice

Like a quince-apple
ripening on a top
branch in a tree top

not noticed by
harvesters or if
not unnoticed, not reached

Second
Voice

Like a hyacinth in
the mountains, trampled
by shepherds until
only a purple stain
remains on the ground

By Sappho[32]

When the Cretan maidens
Dancing up the full moon
Round some fair new altar,
Trample the soft blossoms of fine grass,

There is mirth among them.
Aphrodite's children
Ask her benediction
On their bridals in the summer night.

By Sappho[33]

THE MOTHER

As it came to the dawning I awoke:
     Swift I looked in the Courtyard grey—
There but now her fine sleigh stayed,
     While the prancing horses neighed
That bore my Marusenka away.

"Am I no more your child?" she said,
    "That from your side you send me so
Just ere the coming of the night?
     Give me a friend in this my plight—
My songster Solowi must go.

"For its sweet piping I would hear
    At peep of day to waken me—
She, my new mother, will not call,
     Instead, she slanders—cruel words all—
'Useless this bride as rotten tree!' "

In the green garden is fresh-fallen snow;
Horses are galloping to and fro.

A mother follows the hoof-marks deep:
"My Marusenka, where dost thou sleep?

"Help me, O Lord, her steps to trace!
Home I would take her from this place.

"Come, Marusenka, come to me!
If now ill-treated thou mayst be."

She is not in her small white bed.
She sleeps upon the straw instead.

"In what straw, pray, now lieth she?"
She lieth in the rough barley.

"Whose barley pillows now her breast?"
A neighbor's barley gives her rest.

The Ukrainian wedding song cycle[34]

O Faithless thorn
He has my heart no longer
Yet for his sake I no more see
Mother or brother or any friends
O faithless thorn.

An Indian folksong[35]

The bed on which we used to sit
Touching thigh to thigh
Was made of thin cord
And now that bed is broken
As our companionship is broken
How can that wicked bed be mended?
How can we come together again?
A carpenter will mend that wicked bed
At mother's house we will meet again.

*An Indian folksong: the young bride laments
separation from her sister*[36]

Chapter
Four

Married Life

In the women's wing, Bella's roommates were acting like bridesmaids. She had made her own small hat and veil; Mrs. Zimmerman insisted on giving her a pair of matching gloves; Mrs. Rosen brought a small lapel pin for her blue velvet jacket; and the nurse on duty gave her a white linen handkerchief with blue tatting.

The wedding was in the synagogue of the Home. Children and grandchildren, staff and residents, gathered to hear the vows exchanged . . . to shed a silent tear as the cantor sang the ancient hymns to love. And in each listening heart there was a thrust of anxiety as the rabbi spoke briefly and beautifully of hope.

Bella and Sam moved through the ceremony as if they were dreaming it. Finally, the wedding was over. The wedding guests had danced, and everyone had sung the old Yiddish songs with their mixture of tears and gaiety. Sam's son, Eddie, drove them to the small new apartment which the children had found and furnished for them. Then Eddie kissed them both, and went home.

At last the newlyweds were alone—together. And it was real.

For three years, Sam and Bella lived like everyone else. They shopped and cooked, laughed and cried, were restless and content, took care of each other— and lived, together. Sam shopped and grumbled at the high prices . . . and found all sorts of things to worry and complain about. Bella scolded him and calmed him. They quarreled, made up, and loved. Together.

In good weather, they walked to the sunny park across the street, visiting with other elderly people

in the neighborhood. In bad weather they sat before their television, hoping someone would come in to visit . . . being lonely . . . together.

Three golden years. Pleasant and unpleasant. Then Sam's vision began to fail, and Bella became increasingly frail. They decided to call Mrs. Anton.

They were ready now for her original offer. If she still had room for them, they would like to come back to the Home as a couple to live out the rest of their lives together.

And so they did.

From "Aging: An Album of People Growing Old," *by Shura Saul*[37]

IN PRAISE OF MARRIAGE

Marriage is a sweet state,
I can affirm it by my own experience,
In very truth, I who have a good and wise husband
Whom God helped me to find.
I give thanks to him who will save him for me,
For I can truly feel his great goodness
And for sure the sweet man loves me well.

Throughout that first night in our home,
I could well feel his great goodness,
For he did me no excess
That could hurt me.
But, before it was time to get up,
He kissed me 100 times, this I affirm,
Without exacting further outrage,
And yet for sure the sweet man loves me well.

He used to say to me in his soft language:
"God brought you to me,
Sweet lover, and I think he raised me
To be of use to you."
And then he did not cease to dream
All night, his conduct was so perfect,
Without seeking other excesses.
And yet for sure the sweet man loves me well.

O Princes, yet he drives me mad
When he tells me he is all mine;
He will destroy me with his gentle ways,
And yet for sure the sweet man loves me well.

By the French medieval writer Christine de Pisan[38]

MARRIED LOVE

You and I
Have so much love,
That it
Burns like a fire,
In which we bake a lump of clay
Molded into a figure of you
And a figure of me.
Then we take both of them,
And break them into pieces,
And mix the pieces with water,
And mold again a figure of you,
And a figure of me.
I am in your clay.
You are in my clay.
In life we share a single quilt.
In death we will share one coffin.

By the Chinese poet Kuan Tao-sheng (1262–1319)[39]

THE RIVER-MERCHANT'S WIFE:
A LETTER

While my hair was still cut straight across my forehead
I played about the front gate, pulling flowers.
You came by on bamboo stilts, playing horse,
You walked about my seat, playing with blue plums.
And we went on living in the village of Chokan:
Two small people, without dislike or suspicion.

At fourteen I married My Lord you.
I never laughed, being bashful.
Lowering my head, I looked at the wall.
Called to, a thousand times, I never looked back.

At fifteen I stopped scowling,
I desired my dust to be mingled with yours
Forever and forever, and forever.
Why should I climb the look out?

At sixteen you departed,
You went into far Ku-to-Yen, by the river of
    swirling eddies,
And you have been gone five months.
The monkeys make sorrowful noise overhead.
You dragged your feet when you went out.
By the gate now, the moss is grown, the different
    mosses,
Too deep to clear them away!
The leaves fall early this autumn, in wind.
The paired butterflies are already yellow with August
Over the grass in the West garden,
They hurt me,
I grow older,
If you are coming down through the narrows of the
    river Kiang,
Please let me know beforehand,
And I will come out to meet you,
        As far as Cho-fu-Sa.

An ancient Chinese poem by Rihaku,
translated by Ezra Pound[40]

A FAITHFUL WIFE

You know I have a husband.
Why did you give me these two glowing pearls?
I could acknowledge your love
And sew them on my red dress,
But I come from a noble family,
Courtiers of the Emperor.

My husand is an officer in the Palace Guard.
Of course I realize that your intentions
Are pure as the light of Heaven,
But I have sworn to be true to my husband
In life and in death.
So I must give back your beautiful pearls,
With two tears to match them.
Why didn't I meet you
Before I was married?

By the early Chinese poet Chang Chi[41]

TO THE TUNE "WASHING SILK IN THE STREAM"

The warm rain falls unfeeling
Like scattered silk threads.
The farm boy puts a flower behind his ear
As he carries the new grain
From his little field to the threshing floor.
I got up early to water the field
But he was angry with me
For being too early.
I cooked millet for him

Over a smoky fire
But he was angry because it was too late.
My tender bottom is sore all day long.

*By the eighteenth-century Chinese poet
Ho Shuang-Ch'ing*[42]

A SONG OF WHITE HAIR

My love, like my hair, is pure,
Frosty white like the snow on the mountain
Bright and white like the moon amid the clouds.
But I have discovered
You are of a double mind.
We have come to the breaking point.
Today we pledged each other
In a goblet of wine.
Tomorrow I will walk alone
Beside the moat,
And watch the cold water
Flow East and West,
Lonely, mournful
In the bitter weather.
Why should marriage bring only tears?
All I wanted was a man
With a single heart,
And we would stay together
As our hair turned white,
Not someone always after wriggling fish
With his big bamboo rod.
The integrity of a loyal man
Is beyond the value of money.

By the second-century B.C. poet Chuo-Wen-Chun[43]

BRIDESMAIDS' CAROL I

O Bride brimful of
rosy little loves!

O brightest jewel of
the Queen of Paphos!

Come now
      to your
bedroom to your
bed
    and play there
sweetly   gently
with your bridegroom

And may Hesperus
lead you not at all
unwilling
      until
you stand wondering
lead you not at all
unwilling
      until
you stand wondering
before the silver

Throne of Hera
Queen of Marriage

By Sappho[44]

For twelve years I worshipped Siva, and what is my
    reward?
I have got a hunchback husband for my piety
If my hunchback comes while I am straining rice
He goes all over the house to find me the strainer
If he comes in when I am making the bed
He goes about to find the ghursi
But I'd like to get in an engine-cart
And go back to my mother's house.

You may return to your own country, girl
You may marry another man
But he won't be as good as me.

You may turn out a dark girl
You may turn out a fair girl
But you won't get another blue sambhar like me.

In our town there is a Raja
The great Bir Singh Raja
Who's a hunchback just like me.

An Indian folksong: a woman's lament[45]

PARTING OF A NEWLY
WEDDED COUPLE

A dodder clinging to a flax-plant finds
No long or sure support; marriage that binds
A girl and soldier cannot hold for long.
Such a cruel union is as wrong
As throwing out a girl on the roadside.
It's true that I am legally your bride;
My hair's tied firm, but, ah! I'm brokenhearted:
Married at evening and at morning parted!

Too hurriedly by far our union came.
It's true that we are man and wife in name.
The distance isn't what I have to fear;
The frontier station isn't far from here.
But since our marriage hasn't been fulfilled,
How can the beating of our hearts be stilled?
How can I now sincerely have the right
To be a daughter-in-law? By day and night
My parents guarded me and they did not
Give me away for such a wretched lot
Or think, when I was married, I would then
Be poor and lonely as a dog or hen.

You're marching to the frontier to be slain
While I am stumbling to a world of pain.

To go with you would make our trouble worse
For that would only bring our comrades' curse.
You'd better now forget about your bride,
Putting our tenderness and love aside.
Give yourself to the duties of the war;
That's what you should now be living for.
Love and gentleness are for a wife
And kind thoughts wrong in military life.
Silk clothes so long to weave are worthless now;
I wash the rouge and powder from my brow.
Birds fly in pairs while men feel misery;
Longing alone is left for you and me.

"Parting of a newly wedded couple," by the
Chinese poet Tu Fu (A.D. 712–770)[46]

Ri rina rina wo ri ri nawo rina
Life of my mind, where have you gone to fight?
I change my rings from toe to toe
Khelo khelo khelo
But my bed is lonely
Jhelo jhelo jhelo
Life of my mind, where have you gone?
I said, Don't go, but you would go
Khelo khelo khelo
I change my anklets from foot to foot
Jhelo jhelo jhelo
And change them back again
But my bed is lonely
Khelo khelo khelo
Jhelo jhelo jhelo

An Indian folksong[47]

Who is going to Rai Ratanpur and who is going to Drug?
My brother is going to Rai Ratanpur, my husband's
    going to Drug.

Who will bring you anklets to adorn your heels?
Who will bring a co-wife to live in your house?
Brother will bring anklets to adorn my heels
Husband will bring a co-wife to live in my house.

How will I go with the anklets round my heels?
How will I go with a co-wife in the house?
Laughing I will go with anklets round my heels
Crying I will go with a co wife in the house.

What will I do with the anklets round my heels?
What will I do with the co-wife in my house?
I'll change the anklets for others, parrot
I'll throw the co-wife in the fire, parrot.

An Indian folksong: a wife's lament[48]

Fine clothes have come for you
From your new wife's father
Put them on, put them on
My splendid bridegroom
What a picture you will be
A weeding crow has come for you
From your new wife's father
Put it on, put it on
My splendid bridegroom
What a picture you will be
A fine red turban has come for you

From your new wife's father
Put it on, put it on
My splendid bridegroom
What a picture you will be.

An Indian folksong: the first wife taunts her
husband as he takes another wife[49]

You thatched the roof with leaf and branch
What you searched for, that you found
O that you found, my friend

There are five lemon trees
In that fair beauty's garden
But that fair one is going away
Amuse yourself in counting up the days
Till she return—that fair one's going away.

An Indian folksong: the good wife taunts her
husband, who has fallen in love with a fair neighbor[50]

Digging with my finger, parrot
I sowed the kundru seed
Laden low with fruit, parrot
The shrub bent down to earth
Mother-in-law, give me the golden basket
I'm going to pick the kundru.
For whom will you cook potato and brinjal?
For whom will you curry the kundru?
For my lover I'll cook the potato and brinjal

For my hunchback I'll curry the kundru, parrot
Laughing I'll give it to my lover
Weeping I'll give it to my hunchback, parrot
I'd like to run off in an engine-train
But the love of my hunchback keeps me here, parrot.

An Indian folksong[51]

My dear husband, we are lost.
You are not worth much and I am worth less.

A Spanish proverb[52]

BEFORE THE BIRTH OF ONE OF HER CHILDREN

All things within this fading world hath end,
Adversity doth still our joys attend;
No ties so strong, no friends so dear and sweet,
But with death's parting blow is sure to meet.
The sentence past is most irrevocable,
A common thing, yet oh, inevitable.
How soon, my Dear, death may my steps attend,
How soon't may be thy lot to lose thy friend,
We both are ignorant, yet love bids me
These farewell lines to recommend to thee,
That when that knot's untied that made us one,
I may seem thine, who in effect am none.
And if I see not half my days that's due,
What nature would, God grant to yours and you;

The many faults that well you know I have
Let be interred in my oblivious grave;
If any worth or virtue were in me,
Let that live freshly in thy memory
And when thou feel'st no grief, as I no harms,
Yet love thy dead, who long lay in thine arms.
And when thy loss shall be repaid with gains
Look to my little babes, my dear remains.
And if thou love thyself, or loved'st me,
These O protect from step-dame's injury.
And if chance to thine eyes shall bring this verse,
With some sad sighs honour my absent hearse;
And kiss this paper for thy love's dear sake,
Who with salt tears this last farewell did take.

By Anne Bradstreet (1612—1672)[53]

Chapter
Five

Passionate
Woman

THE LITTLE OLD LADY
IN LAVENDER SILK

I was seventy-seven, come August,
  I shall shortly be losing my bloom;
I've experienced zephyr and raw gust
  and (symbolical) flood and simoom.

When you come to this time of abatement,
  To this passing from Summer to Fall,
It is manners to issue a statement
  As to what you got out of it all.

So I'll say, though reflection unnerves me
  And pronouncements I dodge as I can,
That I think (if my memory serves me)
  There was nothing more fun than a man!

In my youth, when the crescent was too wan
  To embarrass with beams from above,
By the aid of some local Don Juan
  I fell into the habit of love.

And I learned how to kiss and be merry—an
  Education left better unsung.
My neglect of the waters Pierian
  Was a scandal when Grandma was young.

Though the shabby unbalanced the splendid,
  And the bitter outmeasured the sweet,
I should certainly do as I then did,
  Were I given the chance to repeat.

For contrition is hollow and wraithful,
  And regret is no part of my plan,
And I think (if my memory's faithful)
  There was nothing more fun than a man!

By Dorothy Parker[54]

WILD NIGHTS

Wild nights! Wild nights!
Were I with thee,
Wild nights should be
Our Luxury!

Futile the winds
To a heart in port, —
Done with the compass,
Done with the chart.

Rowing in Eden!
Ah! the sea!
Might I but moor
To-night in thee!

By Emily Dickinson[55]

If the arms and the legs of the lover
Hollow about my tender flesh
Such furrows as a liana leaves upon
The tree she loves,

Surely the points of my breasts
On the breast of my lover
Shall be as sharpened bamboo branches
Piercing an elephant.

An Indian folksong[56]

You held my lotus blossom
In your lips and played with the
Pistil. We took one piece of
Magic rhinoceros horn
And could not sleep all night long.
All night the cock's gorgeous crest
Stood erect. All night the bee
Clung trembling to the flower
Stamens. Oh my sweet perfumed
Jewel! I will allow only
My lord to possess my sacred
Lotus pond, and every night
You can make blossom in me
Flowers of fire.

By the Chinese poet Huang O[57]

His teeth are white as curds
His eyes are full of sin
His face is beautiful as a wild creeper
His eyes are full of sin
I am only a bit of cucumber
He is the ghee
To make it palatable
He is the arrow
But he has not destroyed me
His arrow has become the pillar of my house.

An Indian folksong[58]

Raja, my heart is mad for you
I have gone mad for you

But you have left the warm bed in my house
Where will you find such warmth outside?
You have left me all alone
You would eat roots and fruit outside
Come, my madman, let us go together to the forest.

Green is the green hill
Yellow are the bamboos
Green is the kalindar creeper
Karanda flowers are in my hair
Where in the forest will I find my Raja?
My heart burns for him
Where in the forest will I find my madman?

An Indian folksong[59]

BIRTH DANCE, BELLY DANCER

(An Invocation to be chanted to Primitive Music)

All veiled from view
she moves toward the altar.
Unknown features, shadow of death, of
        brows, of eyes,
mouth, lips, teeth of the night,
jaw thrust forward like a pelvis,
navel hidden, mysterious circuit,
electrical plug of the first cries
thrust from the womb.

Now the arms ride like serpents from their
        flesh basket,
beat, caress, nip, shimmer the air with
        their rhythmic pulse.

At last the bloody mystery emerges,
Inch by inch the head appears through the
      lost hymen,
inch by inch her grimace works into a
      smile
as the decked and bejeweled mother
      pushes out her ecstasy.

The child cries: it lives.
Its voice rings in her finger cymbals.
She mends her body, slowly
rises from the floor
as her breasts fill with milk.
She shakes them;
this is food, I am food.
this is food, I am food.

The formless fluid shot into her
has been molded and fired in the secret
      oven of her stomach.

Woman, whose nerve-filled clitoris makes
      her shiver,
woman, who is ecstatic mother of us all,
dance, dance with a fury
around your magic circle of women.
Spin out the time spent locked in your
      own womb,
bloom from the vase of your uterus.
Spiral upward and downward, Lady of
      the Garden.

Belly that invites life to sleep in you,
breasts of mortal ambrosia,
body that is food,
Amazon groin that lit the hearth from
      which you gave

the world its bread,
altar, oven, womb,
table of your belly!

Pagan, Earth Mother,
Witch of Magic Birth,
from whom all suck,
the leaves that flow through the body's
    blood,
the cave of your sex, our home,
the earth of birth,
the birth of earth,
Great Mother.

From a birth dance by
contemporary poet Daniela Gioseffi[60]

come to thy beloved one

BEAUTIFUL BEING   triumphant!

come to Thy sister   come to thy wife
    Arise! Arise! Glorious Brother/
      from thy bier that I may
        hover near thy genital
          forever

Beautiful Boy my brother come to my breasts
    take there of that milk to thy fill
      thy nuts will I guard upon
  nor shall the Fiends of Darkness tear at your Eye

come   to   your   house   come   to   your   house

BEAUTIFUL BEING   ! Boy Body!

    that your cock glide forward in radiance
              to our pavilion

Osiris!

Osiris!

when the Ra- Disc glides onward in the Sun-boat

flamespurts spew off the prow

O may I catch thy spurts o brother

as the shrieking human

catches the sun!

The incantation by Isis for
revival of the dead Osiris[61]

I

I cannot sleep
For the blaze of the full moon.
I thought I heard here and there
A voice calling.
Hopelessly I answer "Yes."
To the empty air.

II

It is night again
I let down my silken hair
Over my shoulders
And open my thighs
Over my lover.
"Tell me, is there any part of me
That is not lovable?"

III

I had not fastened my sash over my gown,
When you asked me to look out the window.

If my skirt fluttered open,
Blame the Spring wind.

By the third–fourth-century
Chinese poet Tzu Yeh[62]

LOVE SONG

I passed by the house of the young man who loves me;
I found the door was open.
He sat at his mother's side,
In the midst of his brothers and sisters.
Everyone who passes in the roadway loves him.
He is a fine young man, a man with no equal,
A love of rare character.
And how he stared out at me as I passed by the house!
(I was walking abroad on my own, for my own enjoyment.)
And how my heart leaped up with love,
My dearest lover, when I set eyes on you!
Ah! If only my mother knew what was in my heart
She would go and visit him in a flash!
O golden goddess, inspire in her this thought!
Oh, how I wish to go to my love,
To embrace him openly in front of his family,
And weep no longer because of people's attitude,
To be happy because everyone knows at last
That he and I are in love with each other.
I would hold a little festival in honour of my goddess!

My heart is on fire with the idea of venturing abroad
    again tonight

In order to catch another glimpse of my lover . . .

A fourteenth-century B.C. poem from North Africa[63]

Ayii, Ayii, Ayii,
I am good looking.
My face is beautiful.
I have long shining hair.
My lips and cheeks are red.
And my nose between my eyes
is flat and well formed.
Ayii, Ayii.

An eastern Eskimo song[64]

TO THE TUNE
"RED EMBROIDERED SHOES"

If you don't know how, why pretend?
Maybe you can fool some girls,
But you can't fool Heaven.
I dreamed you'd play with the
Locust blossom under my green jacket,
Like a eunuch with a courtesan.
But lo and behold
All you can do is mumble.
You've made me all wet and slippery,
But no matter how hard you try
Nothing happens. So stop.
Go and make somebody else
Unsatisfied.

By Huang O[65]

Don't give me food
But give me delight
Let me play with you
Let me play in your court
Let me play in your lap
I am only a blue colt
How can I let you tie me?
You have made a cot
But the strings are loose
You say you love me
But you don't come near me.

*An Indian folksong: the lament of a young girl
married to an elderly man*[66]

SPRING SONG

In the sunny Spring of March and April,
When water and grass are the same color,
I met a young man dallying along the road,
I'm sorry I didn't meet him earlier.

In the sunny Spring of March and April
When water and grass are the same color,
I reach up and pick the flowers from the vines.
Their perfume is like my lover's breath.

Four, now five years, I have expected you.
During this long wait my love
Has turned into sorrow.
I wish we could go away, back to some lonely place,
Where I could give my body
Completely to your embraces.

By the third-century Chinese poet Meng Chu[67]

ONE WAY CONVERSATION

There are many men like you, perhaps
most certainly
most

but even though I've had
an itch for the seven-inch
reach   the hard entry
yet
I cannot despise you!

A woman wants above all
to be touched, caressed,
massaged and kissed
and what she carries away
the next day
is pride of flesh
love of link with man
human to human

O do not be distressed
that you cannot create
the great illusion:
thundering gods
at the womb's intrusion . . .
You have a role
valid as sunshine
of speech as equal
of man in parallel
pain . . . joy . . .
partner to woman
You have a role gently caressing
human to human

By the Canadian poet, Dorothy Livesay[68]

THE DANCE OF THE GREASED WOMEN

(Steingeroll) new signs putting
short putting new signs
signs head stretch out
white dots they feel along the wide bands
twins on a pile say
twins a pile say
senses of the girls yell loud
from the sky loudly to say
then the paved women advance in a straight line
the (wasseralber) walk around
salt lakes with upright shores
(wasseralber) high upright
water plans green of grass come
the torch comes
feet quick come

the women of the past come
thick grass come out of
from thick bushels come outside
on the paths of the gods always to lie
the paving lead them
through the rocks' openings lead (gehne ich)
the paving lead them
woman of the past (me) I sigh after my house
from the deep I wish to return
in joy I sigh after the house
the bushes I sigh after the house
in the throat I desire
in the belly I sigh after the house
in the belly I tremble continuously
in the joy I tremble
in the joy I am in mourning
in the belly I am in mourning
the girls tremble continuously
the fertile girls
flames of fire are bent (over) bent (over)
the rock's edge is vaulted is vaulted
the convoy of the heights is well bent is well bent
the eucalyptus foliage is vaulted is vaulted
the agia's trunk is bent
the agia's trunk is bent
the water is vaulted is vaulted
the course of the river is bent is bent
the tied (Geschwurte) are approaching
The past women advance

The lines advance
walking fast walking in a nearby line

on a pile sit down
on blocks of rocks sit down
the flame of fire advances
the great flame

the paving with wheels approaches
    the flame
Inteer angoulba remains standing motionless
the flame of fire remains standing

A fertility dance of southern Africa[69]

Oh,
I am thinking
Oh,
I am thinking
I have found
my lover.
Oh,
I think it is so.

A Chippewa song[70]

TO THE TUNE
"A WATERED SILK DRESS"

The hardest thing in the world
Is to reveal a hidden love.
I swallow my tears
But still they come.
I twist the faded flowers of my hands
And lean speechless against my screen.
When I look in the mirror
My wasted figure frightens me.
Not a springlike face.
Not an autumnal face.
Is this me? Shuang-ch'ing?

By Ho Shuang-Ch'ing[71]

MEN'S IMPOTENCE

Maybe—yes
it doesn't matter.
Maybe—yes.
I'll just sing about a man,
"The One at Boiling-Point,"
who sat tight-lipped and frightened
among women.

Maybe—yes
it doesn't matter.
Maybe—yes.
I'll just sing about a man,
"The Reindeer-Belly,"
who sat tight-lipped and frightened
among women.
His eyes augured ill,
curved like a horn
to carve into an eeling-fork.

Maybe—yes
it doesn't matter.
Maybe-yes.
I'll just sing about a man,
"The Axe,"
who sat tight-lipped and frightened,
far, far away from people,
in solitude.

Maybe—yes
it doesn't matter.
Maybe—yes.
My tongue can only put together words
to make a little song.
A mouth, a little mouth,
can that be dangerous?

A little mouth,
that curves down at the corners
like a stick,
bent to form a kayak's rib.

An Eskimo song[72]

ON THE SLOPE OF HUA MOUNTAIN

O Flowery Mountain slopes,
Now that my lover is dead
How can I live out my lonely life?

O my lover, if you still love me,
Open your sealed coffin for me,
And take me with you.

Why is it, with the world full of men
I am desolated, and long only for you?

I wish I were the ivy,
climbing high in the pine tree,
And you were the moving clouds,
So we could see each other
As you pass by.

An anonymous Chinese poem, fifth century A.D.[73]

FOR THE COURTESAN CH'ING LIN

On your slender body
Your jade and coral girdle ornaments chime
Like those of a celestial companion
Come from the Green Jade City of Heaven.
One smile from you when we meet,
And I become speechless and forget every word.
For too long you have gathered flowers,
And leaned against the bamboos,
Your green sleeves growing cold,
In your desert valley:
I can visualize you all alone,
A girl harboring her cryptic thoughts.

You glow like a perfumed lamp
In the gathering shadows.
We play wine games
And recite each other's poems.
Then you sing "Rembering South of the River"
With its heart breaking verses. Then
We paint each other's beautiful eyebrows.
I want to possess you completely—
Your jade body
And your promised heart.
It is Spring.
Vast mists cover the Five Lakes.
My dear, let me buy a red painted boat
And carry you away.

*By the nineteenth-century Chinese
lesbian poet Wu Tsao*[74]

LOVE-MAKING

Ajaija-ja,
my playmate
ja-ja-jai-ja,
fingers me
between the legs,
hajaijaja,
she gives her body
haijaijaja-jaja—
and tears the leather bracelets
from my wrists.

An Eskimo song[75]

JOY

Joy shakes me like the wind that lifts a sail,
Like the roistering wind
That laughs through stalwart pines.
It floods me like the sun
On rain-drenched trees
That flash with silver and green.

I abandon myself to joy—
I laugh—I sing.
Too long have I walked a desolate way,
Too long stumbled down a maze
Bewildered.

By the American poet Clarissa Scott Delany[76]

Love has come to me, the kind I am far more ashamed
To conceal than to reveal to anyone.
Cytherea, won over by my Muses' prayers,
Has brought him to me and placed him in my arms.
Venus has fulfilled her promises. Let my joys
Be told by those said to lack joys of their own.
I won't entrust my thoughts to tablets under seal
For fear that someone may read them before he does.
But I'm glad I've erred; falsely posing disgusts me:
Let me be called worthy, him worthy as well.

By the Greek poet Sulpicia, 14 B.C. [77]

The tears gush from my eyes,
My eyelashes are wet with tears;
But stay my tears within,
Lest you should be called mine.
Alas! I am betrothed (literally "my hands are bound"),
It is for Te Maunu,
That my love devours me.
But I may weep indeed,
Beloved one for thee.
Like Tinirau's lament
For his favorite pet,
Tutunui,
Which was slain by Ngae.
Alas!

A primitive American Indian folk poem
first published in 1903 [78]

Dearest, I know that thy body is but transitory; that
the kindled life, thy shining eyes, shall be quenched
by the touch of death, I know; that this thy body,
the meeting place of all beauty, in seeing which
I count my life well-lived, shall become but a heap
of bones, I know.

Yet I love thy body. Day by day afresh through it have
I satisfied a woman's love and desire by serving thy
feet and worshipping thee. On days of good omen
I have decked thee with a flower-garland; on days of
woe I have wiped away with my sari end thy tears of
grief.

O my lord, I know that thy soul is with the Everlasting
One, yet waking suddenly some nights I have wept
in loneliness, thinking how thou didst drive away
my fear, clasping me to thy breast. And so I count
thy body as the chief goal of my love, as very heaven.

A poem by a Bengali woman[79]

I have painted my eyes,
I have girded my hips.
I am full of the desire of love.
O my handsome lover!
I shall go behind the wall,
And wearing an apron,
I shall help him paint.
I shall mix his plaster
To repair his house.
O my beautiful, slim lover!
I am going to use a thaler
To buy me a kerchief of silk.
I shall put on my best,
To be with him.
O my handsome,
My slim and graceful lover!

A love song from Guinea [80]

I know not whether thou has been absent:
I lie down with thee, I rise up with thee,
In my dreams thou art with me.
If my eardrops tremble in my ears,
I know it is thou moving within my heart.

An Aztec love song sung by an Indian girl in
the Sierra of Ramaulipas [81]

1.

Now you love me;
Now you admire me,
but you threw me away
like something that tasted bad.
You treated me as if I were a rotten fish.
Now my old grandmother takes her dry
blackberries and puts them under her blanket.

2.

I though you were good.
I thought you were like silver;
You are lead.

You see me high up on the mountain.
I walk through the sun;
I am sunlight myself.

Two divorce songs of the British Columbia Indians [82]

Apart from Rama, sleep does not come to me,
Through the sufferings of separation no sleep comes,
And the fire of love is kindled.

Without the light of my beloved, the temple is dark;
The lamp does not please me.
Apart from my beloved, I feel very lonely;
The night is passed in waking
When will my beloved come home?

Excerpt by a medieval Hindi poet[83]

Chapter
Six

Woman's Body:
The Sexual Center

Oh, golden flower opened up
> she is our mother
whose thighs are holy
> whose face is a dark mask.
She came from Tamoanchan,
> the first place
where all descended
> where all was born.
Oh, golden flower flowered
> she is our mother
whose thighs are holy
> whose face is a dark mask.
She came from Tamoanchan

Oh, white flower opened up
> she is our mother
whose thighs are holy
> whose face is a dark mask.
She came from Tamoanchan,
> the first place
where all descended
> where all was born.
Oh, white flower flowered
> she is our mother
whose thighs are holy
> whose face is a dark mask.
She came from Tamoanchan.

She lights on the round cactus,
> she is our mother
the dark obsidian butterfly.
> Oh, we saw her as we
> wandered
Across the Nine Plains,
> she fed herself with deers'
> hearts.

She is our mother,
                    the goddess earth.
                                    She is dressed
in plumes
                    she is smeared with clay.
In all four directions of wind
                                    the arrows are broken.
They saw you as a deer
                    in the barren land.
those two men, Xiuhnel and Mimich.

An Aztec poem to the mother of the gods[84]

Yes my child come do the birth dance
Proud animal not caught in a trap
Come here and join the birth dance
So your god will give you a child.
Yes my child come join the birth dance
So God will give you a child.

An Igbo prayer for fertility[85]

Give a seat to your visitor
So will you be honoured
Give prepared supari to your own mate
Pray that a barren woman may have a child
O brother, I have thought and thought
I have asked my heart
By this anxious thought my life has wept.

*An Indian folksong: a prayer
for the barren woman*[86]

The water from the little fall doth shine
As on the forelock of my hair it stays;
The sunbeams of the dawn outspreading nine,
In thy name, God of life, thy servant prays;
Away the red miscarriage from me raise;
The woman's hope of hurrying is mine.

A woman's prayer from the isle of Skye in the
Western Highlands of Scotland[87]

PRAYER OF AN OVULATING FEMALE

I bring no throat-slit kid
no heart-scooped victim
no captive decapitated
and no self-scourged flesh.

I bring you, Domina,
Mother of women,
a calendula in a pot
a candle and a peach
an egg and a
split condom.

Ave Mater
Mulierum!
may no blood flow
nec in caelo
nec in terra
except according
to the calendar.

By Dilys Laing (1906 – 1960)[88]

Kangiak, while you take me for a fool,
I take you also for a fool.
Kangiak, take nothing on yourself.
Take three women to yourself.
One of them can get no children.
You must try to get her.
You must use her as usual.
It is not in the least difficult.

The agonies of the neglected barren Eskimo woman[89]

Then . . . she (Ninmah) made into a woman who
    cannot give birth.
Enki upon seeing the woman who cannot give birth,
Decreed her fate, destined her to be stationed in
the "woman house."

*A Sumerian myth concerning
the creation of the barren woman*[90]

Into view on the horizon came two figures, moving
very slowly. I went on with my pounding. The figures
grew larger every time I looked up, and then when
they were still a fair distance away I recognized my
daughter. I had seen her only once since her marriage,
and since then over a year had passed.

They approached slowly, as if their feet were
somehow weighted. Something is wrong, I thought.
Young people should not walk thus. And when I saw
their faces the words of welcome I had ready died
unuttered.

In silence Ira knelt at my feet. I raised her up quickly, with hammering heart. "Let us go in," I said. "You must be tired."

Ira entered obediently. Her husband stood stiffly outside.

"Mother-in-law," he said, "I intend no discourtesy, but this is no ordinary visit. You gave me your daughter in marriage. I have brought her back to you. She is a barren woman."

"You have not been married long," I said with dry lips. "She may yet conceive."

"I have waited five years," he replied. "She has not borne in her first blooming, who can say she will conceive later. I need sons."

Ira was sitting with her face in her arms. She looked up, and her mouth moved a little, loosely, as if she had no control over her lips. She was lovely still, but strain and hopelessness had shadowed her eyes and lined her forehead. She seemed to back away as I went to her.

"Leave me alone, Mother. I have seen this coming for a long time. The reality is much easier to bear than the imaginings. At least now there is no more fear, no more necessity for lies and concealment."

From Nectar in a Sieve, *by Kamela Markandaya, a modern Indian writer*[91]

THE ABORTION

1.

East, west, north, south
Tell me in which river
We shall put away the child
With rotting thatch below it
And jungly silk above
We will have it put away
You at the lower steps
I at the upper
We will wash and go to our homes
You by the lower path
I by the upper
We will go to our homes.

2.

O my love
My mind has broken
For the spring has ceased its flow
In the gully by the plantain
Drink cups of medicine
Swallow down some pills
Like a black cow
That has never had a calf
You will again be neat and trim.

3.

Like a bone
Was the first child born
And the white ants have eaten it
O my love, do not weep
Do not mourn
We two are here
And the white ants have eaten it.

4.

The field has not been ploughed
The field is full of sand
Little grandson
Why do you linger?
From a still unmarried girl
A two-months child has slipped
And that is why they stare.

5

You by the village street
I by the track in the garden
We will take the child away
To the right is a bent tree
To the left is a stump
O my love
We will bury it between them.

6.

In the unploughed rice field, elder brother
What birds are hovering?
At midnight, the headman's middle daughter
Has taken it away
They are tearing the after-birth to pieces.

A poem from India: Santal[92]

I was forty, and I remember greeting the certitude of the belated child's presence with serious mistrust, while saying nothing about it. Physical apprehension had nothing to do with my behavior; I was simply afraid that at my age I would not know how to give a child the proper love and care, devotion and understanding. Love—so I believed—had already hurt me a great deal by monopolizing me for the past twenty years.

It is neither wise nor good to start a child with too much thought. Little used to worrying about the future, I found myself for the first time preparing for an exact date that it would have been quite enough to think about only four weeks beforehand. I meditated, I tried to think clearly and reasonably, but I was struck by the recollection that intelligent cats are usually bad mothers, sinning by inadvertence or by excess of zeal, constantly moving their kittens from place to place, holding them by the nape of the neck, pinched between their teeth, hesitating where to deposit them. What a comfortable nest that sagging seat of an armchair! However, less so than under the down quilt, perhaps? But surely the acme of comfort would be the second drawer of the commode?

During the first three months I told almost no one of my condition or my worries. I did tell Charles Sauerwein and was struck by his comment. "Do you know what you're doing?" he exclaimed. "You're behaving as a man would, you're having a masculine pregnancy! You must take it more lightheartedly than this. Come, put on your hat, we'll go to the Poirée-Blanche and have some strawberry ice cream."

Fortunately I changed, without realizing it at first. Soon everyone around me began to exclaim how well I looked and how cheerful I was. The half-ridden and

involuntary smile of pregnant women showed even
through my makeup as the Optimistic Owl—for I was
serenely continuing to play my part in *L'Oiseau de
Nuit*, which involved some skillful pugilistics, mean
uppercuts, and some rough and tumble clinches, on
the table, under the table . . . A masculine pregnancy?
Yes, and one might even say the pregnancy of a
champion, for I had the taut, well-muscled body of
an athlete . . .

Colette describing her first pregnancy at 40[93]

WITH CHILD

Now I am slow and placid, fond of sun,
Like a sleek beast, or a worn one:
No slim and languid girl—not glad
With the windy trip I once had,
But velvet-footed, musing of my own,
Torpid, mellow, stupid as a stone.
You cleft me with your beauty's pulse, and now
Your pulse has taken body. Care not how
The old grace goes, how heavy I am grown,
Big with this loneliness, how you alone
Ponder our love. Touch my feet and feel
How earth tingles, teeming at my heel!
Earth's urge, not mine—my little death, not hers;
And the pure beauty yearns and stirs.
It does not heed our ecstasies, it turns
With secrets of its own, its own concerns,
Toward a windy world of its own, toward stark
And solitary places. In the dark,
Defiant even now, it tugs and moans
To be untangled from these mother's bones.

*By the American poet
Genevieve Taggard (1894—1948)*[94]

O Mother, do not again give me a woman's birth
From the beginning there is great suffering for women
O Mother, in the shadow of the twelfth year
My head was found defiled and soon I was pregnant
The first month is over, Mother
The blood gathers drop by drop
The second month is over, Mother
In the shadow of the third month
My body is yellow as haldi
And I long for buttermilk
My hands and feet are heavy as earth
I cannot bear the sun
O Mother, do not again give me a woman's birth
The fourth month is over, Mother
In the fifth month the life comes phud phud
My body feels lighter than before
In the shadow of the sixth month
My body begins to look big
My mind thinks, what shall I eat
And what shall I avoid?
But to no one can I tell my desire
The seventh month is over, Mother
The child born in the seventh month
Can hardly live
The child born in the eighth month
is sure to die
Under the shadow of the ninth month
The children of all the world are born.

An Indian pregnancy song lamenting the fate
of being a woman[95]

THE MOTHERS

O pregnant womanhood that scarce can drag
thy weary ripeness round the allotted track,
    and soon would rest thee on unkindly bench,
    closely foregathering like affrighted sheep;

In these thy days of fruitfulness thou'rt robbed
of those dear joys that should thy state enrich,
making thy presence blossom like thy womb
and with a sweet expectancy thy thoughts to leap;
a changeless sadness girdles thee about;
each sister whispers faltering unto each
and with wan smiles and pleading arms outstretched,
thou turn'st towards youngling babes, born 'twixt
    these walls,
pledges to thee that thy regretful fruit
will not be monstrous though in prison grown.

*By Sylvia Pankhurst, written
during her jail term*[96]

I heard a buzzing, and then my father's voice.
"Vanessa? Listen, sweetheart, tell your mother I won't
be home for a while yet. I'll have dinner here. And
tell her she's to go home early and get to bed. How
is she?"

"She's okay." But I was immediately alert. "Why?
What was the matter with her?"

"Nothing. But you be sure to tell her, eh?"

I ran upstairs and repeated what he had said. Aunt
Edna looked at my mother oddly.

"Beth?"

"It wasn't anything," my mother said quickly. "Only the merest speck. You know how Ewen fusses."

"No, he doesn't," Aunt Edna said. "You tell me the truth this minute, Beth."

My mother's voice was slow and without expression.

"All right, then. It was a pretty near thing. I suppose. It happened on Tuesday, after I'd been doing the rugs. That's why I didn't want to tell you. You don't need to say it was my own fault. I know it. But I'd been feeling perfectly well, Edna. Really I had."

She looked up at Aunt Edna, and there was something in her eyes I had not seen before, some mute appeal.

"If I'd lost it, I'd never have forgiven myself. I didn't do it on purpose, Edna."

"You don't have to tell me that," Aunt Edna cried. "Don't you think I know?"

And then, strangely, while I sat on the cedar chest and watched, only partially knowing and yet bound somehow to them, they hugged each other tightly and I saw the tears on both their faces although they were not making a sound.

"Mercy," my mother said at last, "my nose is shining like a beacon—where's your powder?"

By the contemporary Canadian author Margaret Laurence[97]

Don't scold me, grannie
I can't bear this rice-gruel
I want some kudai
Some dallia-pej and khichri.

Three months have gone, child
There are no signs yet
If it is a boy
In five months you'll know
If it is a girl
In four months it quivers bog big
Don't go much to the bazaar
There are ghosts along the road.

An Indian folksong[98]

NINE POEMS FOR THE UNBORN CHILD

v

Eating sleep, eating sunlight, eating meat,
Lying in the sun to stare
At deliverance, the rapid cloud,
Gull-wing opposing sun-bright wind,
I see the born who dare
Walk on green, walk against blue,
Move in the nightlong flare
Of love on darkness, traveling
Among the rings of light to simple light,
From nowhere to nowhere.
And in my body feel the seasons grown.
Who is it in the dim room? Who is there?

viii

Child who within me gives me dreams and sleep,
Your sleep, your dreams; you hold me in your flesh

Including me where nothing has included
Until I said: I will include, will wish
And in my belly be a birth, will keep
All delicacy, all delight unclouded.

Dreams of an unborn child move through my dreams,
The sun is not alone in making fire and wave
Find meeting-place, for flesh and future meet,
The seal in the green wave like you in me,
Child. My book at night full of your dreams,
Sleep coming by day as strong as sun on me,
Coming with sun dreams where leaves and rivers meet,
And I at last alive sunlight and wave.

From Nine Poems for the Unborn Child,
by Muriel Rukeyser (1913)[99]

In the house with the tortoise chair
    she will give birth to the pearl
            to the beautiful feather

in the house of the goddess who sits on a tortoise
    she will give birth to the necklace of pearls
            to the beautiful feathers we are

there she sits on the tortoise
    swelling to give us birth

on your way on your way
    child be on your way to me here
            you whom I made new

come here child   come be pearl
            be beautiful feather

An Aztec poem to ease birth[100]

It is that, in fact, that first among others, He
caused the body of our mother—the woman—to
be of great worth and honor. He purposed that
she shall be endowed and entrusted with the
duties pertaining to the birth—the becoming—
of men, and that she shall, in the next place, circle
around the fire in preparing food—that she shall
have the care of all that is planted by which life
is sustained and supported, and so the power to
breathe is fortified; and moreover that the
warriors shall be her assistants.

An Iroquois ritual[101]

She says these words,   made this remark:
"Come, Nature, to protect me,   to help me,
    merciful one,
in these severe labors,   in these very difficult times.
Free the maid from her torment,   the woman from
    her labor pains
so that she may not lapse into agony   nor pine away
    in agony."

Then, after she got to her destination,   she uttered
    these words:
"Breathe, good horse,   puff, draft colt,
puff bath vapor,   send warm sauna steam
That I, poor wretch, may get relief.   I, anguished one,
    need help."
The good horse breathed,   the draft colt gave deep
    puffs
on the belly of the anguished girl.   By as much as
    the horse breathes,

by so much was sauna vapor produced,   water thrown
    and vapor produced.
Marjatta, lowly maiden,   pure little maid,
bathed all she wanted in the bathhouse, all she
    cared to in the steam.
There she produced a little boy,   bore an innocent
    child
on the hay by the horse,   in the shaggy one's manger.
She washed her little son,   wrapped him in his
    swaddling clothes,
took the boy on her knees,   fixed up the child
    on her lap.
She kept her son out of sight,   cared for her beauty,
There she produced a little boy,   bore an innocent
    child
on the hay by the horse,   in the shaggy one's manger.
She washed her little son,   wrapped him in his
    swaddling clothes,
took the boy on her knees,   fixed up the child on
    her lap.
She kept her son out of sight,   cared for her beauty,
her golden apple, her silver staff.
She nursed him in her arms,   turned him over in
    her hands.
She set the boy on her knees,   the child on her lap,
began to groom his head,   to comb his hair.

*A prayer for labor pains, from the
Finnish Kalevala* [102]

From the heart of Earth, by means of yellow pollen
    blessing is extended.
From the Heart of Sky, by means of blue pollen blessing
    is extended.
On top of a pollen floor may I there in blessing
    [successfully] give birth!
On top of a floor of fabrics may I there in blessing
    give birth!
As collected water flows ahead of it [the child],
    whereby blessing moves along ahead of it, may I
    there in blessing give birth!
Thereby without hesitating, thereby with its mind
    straightened, thereby with its travel means straight-
    ened, thereby without its sting, may I there in
    blessing give birth!
As water's child flows behind it whereby blessing
    moves along behind it may I there in blessing give
    birth!
Thereby without hesitating, thereby with its mind
    straightened, thereby with its travel means
    straightened, thereby without its sting, may I there
    in blessing [successfully] give birth!
With pollen moving around it, with blessing extending
    from it by means of pollen, may I in blessing give
    birth!
May I give birth to Pollen Boy, may I give birth to
    Cornbeetle Boy, may I give birth to Long-life Boy,
    may I give birth to Happiness Boy!
With long life-happiness surrounding me may I in
    blessing give birth! May I quickly give birth!
In blessing may I arise again, in blessing may I recover,
    as one who is long life-happiness may I live on!
Before me may it be blessed, behind me . . ., below me
    . . . above me . . ., in all my surroundings may it
    be blessed, may my speech be blessed! It has

become blessed again, it has become blessed again,
it has become blessed again, it has become blessed
again!

A Navaho ritual for giving birth[103]

BRIDE THE AID-WOMAN

There came to me assistance,
Mary fair and Bride;
As Anna bore Mary,
As Mary bore Christ,
As Eile bore John the Baptist
Without flaw in him,
Aid thou me in mine unbearing,
 Aid me, O Bride!

As Christ was conceived of Mary
Full perfect on every hand,
Assist thou me, foster-mother,
The conception to bring from the bone;
And as thou didst aid the Virgin of joy,
Without gold, without corn, without kine,
Aid thou me, great is my sickness,
 Aid me, O Bride.

A Gaelic prayer to St. Bridgit or Bride[104]

Of the [seven] and seven mother-wombs, seven
 brought forth males, [Seven] brought forth females.
The Mother-Womb, the creatress of destiny,
In pairs she completed them,

In pairs she completed before her.
The forms of the people Mami forms.
In the house of the bearing woman in travail,
    Seven days shall the brick lie.
. . . from the house of Mah, the wise Mami.
The vexed one shall rejoice in the house of the one
  in travail.
As the Bearing One gives birth,
May the mother of the child bring forth by [her]self.

An Assyrian version of an ancient Babylonian
childbirth incantation [105]

PARTURITION

I am the centre
Of a circle of pain
Exceeding its boundaries in every direction
The business of the bland sun
Has no affair with me
In my congested cosmos of agony
From which there is no escape
On infinitely prolonged nerve-vibrations
Or in contraction
To the pin-point nucleus of being
Locate an irritation   without
It is   within
Within
It is without.
The sensitized area
Is identical   with the extensity
of intension

I am the false quantity
In the harmony of physiological potentiality
To which
Gaining self-control
I should be consonant
In time

Pain is no stronger than the resisting force
Pain calls up in me
The struggle is equal
I am climbing a distorted mountain of agony
Incidentally with the exhaustion of control
I reach the summit
And gradually subside into anticipation of
Repose
Which never comes.
For another mountain is growing up
Which   goaded by the unavoidable
I must traverse
Traversing myself

Something in the delirium of night-hours
Confuses while intensifying sensibility
Blurring spatial contours
So aiding elusion of the circumscribed
That the gurgling of a crucified wild beast
Comes from so far away
And the foam on the stretched muscles of a mouth
Is no part of myself
There is a climax in sensibility
When pain surpassing itself
Becomes exotic
And the ego succeeds in unifying the positive and
    negative poles of sensation.
Uniting the opposing and resisting forces
In lascivious revelation

Excerpts from Parturition,
by Mina Loy (1882–1966)[106]

O Ukko, god on high,   come look here,
look closely,   come secretly to the sauna,
secretly into the little room   without the door's
    creaking,
without the hinges' squeaking.   I will grease the
    door with beer.
wet the hinges with table beer   so that the door will
    not creak
nor the hinges squeak.   Go quickly, get there
    without delay
in this severe pain,   in the hard labor pains.
Open the fleshy chest,   draw the bolt of bone
for a big one to go through, a small one to go
    through   for a feeble one to proceed,
for a maiden to get free of her torment,   a woman
    free of her belly cramps.

Maidenly old woman, Nature Spirit, golden woman,
    fair one,
you who are the oldest of women,   first mother
    among humans!
Run into the sea up to your knees,   into the billows
    up to your belt buckle.
Take some slaver from a ruff,   some slime from a cusk
with which to anoint the spaces between the
    bones,   with which to stroke along the sides,
to rub the back.   You rid the maiden of her torment,
the woman of her belly cramps   in this severe pain,
in the hard labor pains.

                        Pain Spirit, mistress of pain,
come here with swift-moving shoes,   flutter along in
    fine skirts;
go proudly in black stockings,   walk with white stockings
to seize fast the pains, to silence the injuries

or death will come,   departure of the spirit draw near
in this agonizing pain,   in this hard labor.

*A charm for a woman in labor
in the Finnish Kalevala*[107]

When the rain is raining,
I am under the eave;
I am afraid of lightning,
I am even alarmed by drizzle.
When a woman gives birth,
I am under the galanta [threshold between the front
    and back rooms],
Afraid of her labor,
Alarmed by her pushing.
Atete . . .
When in pain, you clutched at the grass;
When pushing, you clutched at the wall;
After birth, you caught your child.
Maram gave you a present;
For your pain you now have a baby;
Instead of pain, the baby is yours.

Birth song of the women of the Macha Galla[108]

PARTURITION

LIFE
A leap with nature
Into the essence
Of unpredicted Maternity

Against my thigh
Touch or infinitesimal motion
Scarcely perceptible
Undulation

Warmth moisture
Stir of incipient life
Precipitating into me
The contents of the universe
Mother I am
Identical
With infinite Maternity
　　Indivisible
　　Acutely
　　I am absorbed
　　Into
The was—is—ever—shall—be
Of cosmic reproductivity

Rises from the subconscious
Impression of a cat
With blind kittens
Among her legs
Same undulating life-stir
I am that cat

Rises from the sub-conscious
Impression of small animal carcass
Covered with blue-bottles
—Epicurean—
And through the insects
Waves that same undulation of living
Death
Life
I am knowing
All about
　　Unfolding

The next morning
Each woman-of-the-people
Tip-toeing the red pile of the carpet
Doing hushed service
Each woman-of-the-people
Wearing a halo
Of which she is sublimely unaware

From Parturition *by Mina Loy (1882 – 1966)*[109]

All Igbo come and see that my
   child has given birth
All Igbo come and see that my
   child has given birth
All Igbo come and see that my
   child has given birth
If she had killed the child in
   delivery they would all have
   heard
Excellent young woman she
delivered a child.

An Igbo song in praise of birth[110]

The nurses begin to talk again. I say: let me alone.
I put my two hands on my stomach and very softly,
with the tips of my fingers I drum drum drum drum
drum drum on my stomach in circles. Around,

around, softly, with eyes open in great serenity. The doctor comes near with amazement on his face. The nurses are silent. Drum drum drum drum drum drum in soft circles, soft quiet circles. Like a savage. The mystery. Eyes open, nerves begin to shiver . . . a mysterious agitation. I hear the ticking of the clock . . . inexorably, separately. The little nerves awake, stir. But my hands are so weary, so weary, they will fall off. The womb is stirring and dilating. Drum drum drum drum drum. I am ready! The nurse presses her knee on my stomach. There is blood in my eyes. A tunnel. I push into this tunnel, I bite my lips and push. There is a fire and flesh ripping and no air. Out of the tunnel! All my blood is spiling out. Push! Push! Push! It is coming! It is coming! It is coming! I feel the slipperiness, the sudden deliverance, the weight is gone. Darkness. I hear voices. I open my eyes. I hear them saying: "It was a girl. Better not show it to her." All my strength returns. I sit up. The doctor shouts: "Don't sit up!"

"Show me the child!"

"Don't show it," says the nurse, "it will be bad for her." The nurses try to make me lie down. My heart is beating so loud I can hardly hear myself repeating: "Show it to me." The doctor holds it up. It looks dark and small, like a diminutive man. But it is a little girl. It has long eyelashes on its closed eyes, it is perfectly made, and all glistening with the waters of the womb.

Anais Nin's experience of the stillbirth of a daughter [111]

MATERNITY

One wept whose only child was dead
   New-born, ten years ago.
"Weep not; he is in bliss," they said.
   She answered, "Even so,

"Ten years ago was born in pain
   A child, not now forlorn.
But oh, ten years ago, in vain,
   A mother, a mother was born."

By Alice Meynell (1847 – 1923)[112]

SONG FOR THE NEWBORN

Newborn, on the naked sand
Nakedly lay it.
Next to the earth mother,
That it may know her;
Having good thoughts of her, the food giver.

Newborn, we tenderly
In our arms take it,
Making good thoughts.
House-god, be entreated,
That it may grow from childhood to manhood,
Happy, contented;
Beautifully walking
The trail to old age.
Having good thoughts of the earth its mother,
That she may give it the fruits of her being.

Newborn, on the naked sand
Nakedly lay it.

To be sung by the one who first takes
the child from its mother, from the Grande Pueblos [113]

O woman with child, it was good you gave birth.
O woman with child, it was good you gave birth.
Woman with child, kaya [a fragrant plant] is on
    your heels.
Woman with child, it was good you gave birth.
Woman with child, it was good you gave birth.
Mother, may your child be healthy.
Woman with child, it was good you gave birth.
Woman with child, it was good you gave birth.
Woman with child, boooko at the river,
When you are wet, you are sprouting.
Barren woman, kusaye [a fragrant tree], on the hill,
You smell good, but you are dry.
O lying-in woman, your clothes are kobbo [ensete,
    a plant with a bad smell],
But honor adorns your borro [rear wall of house,
    hence the back room].
Your husband stands at the door laughing.
Maram adorned your borro [with a child].
O Maram, let me be strong for you,
Let me be pleasing to you,
Let me gain strength for you.
O Maram, I have value in your eyes;
I am sleeping without clothes,
But for you I'll put on my kafana.
O Maram, for you I am tied,
For you I sleep in the center,
For you I stay where I am.

The hunter returns to the wilderness,
And the lying-in woman to labor.
The hunter should have his spoil;
With a buffalo tail he is worth seeing.
The woman should have her spoil;
With a child she is worth seeing.
Woman with child, it was good you gave birth.
Woman with child, it was good you gave birth.

Birth song for soloist and chorus of the
women of the Macha Galla[114]

THE BIRTH IN A NARROW ROOM

Weeps out of Kansas country something new.
Blurred and stupendous. Wanted and unplanned.
   Winks.   Twines, and weakly winks
Upon the milk-glass fruit bowl, iron pot,
The bashful china child tipping forever
Yellow apron and spilling pretty cherries.

Now, weeks and years will go before she thinks
"How pinch is my room! how can I breathe!
I am not anything and I have got
Not anything, or anything to do!"—
But prances nevertheless with gods and fairies
Blithely about the pump and then beneath
The elms and grapevines, then in darling endeavor
By privy foyer, where the screenings stand
And where the bugs buzz by in private cars
Across old peach cans and old jelly jars.

by the Black American poet
Gwendolyn Brooks (1917—   )[115]

Ah, but the baby! The baby was astonishing; formed like a Cupid, with blue eyes and long brown hair, that afterwards fell out and gave place to golden curls. And miracle of miracles, that mouth sought my breast and bit with toothless gums, and pulled and drank the milk that gushed forth . . .

Oh, women, what is the good of us learning to become lawyers, painters, or sculptors, when this miracle exists? Now I knew this tremendous love, surpassing the love of man. I was stretched and bleeding, torn and helpless, while the little being sucked and howled. Life, life, life! Give me life." Oh, where was my Art? My Art or any Art? What did I care for Art? I felt I was a God, superior to any artist.

During the first weeks, I used to lie long hours with the baby in my arms, watching her asleep; sometimes catching a gaze from her eyes; feeling very near the edge, the mystery, perhaps the knowledge of life. This soul in the newly created body which answered my gaze with such apparently old eyes — the eyes of Eternity—gazing into mine with love. Love, perhaps, was the answer of all. What words could describe this joy? What wonder that I, who am not a writer, cannot find any words at all!

From My Life, *by Isadora Duncan*[116]

WAITING FOR MOTHER

There are many people returning from the market
The mother of the child has a god of her own
   to protect her.
She will come home for us, a-running
And carrying what she bought.
What will she bring from the market?
She will trade salt, and from the profit
She will buy some meat.
When she returns, she will drop it on the floor.
She will say: "Let me have my baby!"
And she will kiss you
And she will carry you
And she will give you her breast.

An African poem[117]

Thy mother is the Great Wild Cow, living
   in Nekheb,
The White Crown, the Royal Headdress,
With the two tall feathers,
With the two pendulous breasts.
She will suckle thee,
She will not wean thee

My son Pepi, so she said,
Take my breast that thou mayest drink, so she said;
So that thou livest (again), so that thou becomest
   small (again), so she said;
Thou wilt go forth to heaven like the falcons;
Thy pinions will be like those of geese, so she said

Excerpts from an ancient Near Eastern text[118]

NIGHT FEEDING

Deeper than sleep but not so deep as death
I lay there dreaming and my magic head
remembered and forgot.   On first cry I
remembered and forgot and did believe.

I knew love and I knew evil:
woke to the burning song and the tree burning blind,
despair of our days and the calm milk-giver who
knows sleep, knows growth, the sex of fire and grass,
renewal of all waters and the time of the stars
and the black snake with gold bones.

Black sleeps, gold burns;   on second cry I woke
fully and gave to feed and fed on feeding.
Gold seed, green pain, my wizards in the earth
walked through the house, black in the morning dark.
Shadows grew in my veins, my bright belief,
my head of dreams deeper than night and sleep.
Voices of all black animals crying to drink,
cries of all birth arise, simple as we,
found in the leaves, in clouds and dark, in dream,
deep as this hour, ready again to sleep.

By Muriel Rukeyser[119]

When the child in your womb
Already leaps and moves,
Let not your look stop,
Young mother,
Let not your look stop
On the trailing tortoise,
Which moves its scales on the pathway!
Look not at the leper who strays in the village!

Let your child,
Young mother,
Let the child who comes forth from your womb
Not see, as he sucks the nourishing milk,
Not see either the tortoise which moves its scales on
    the pathway,
Or the leper who strays in the village.

*A Gabon pygmy song of advice to protect the
child before and after birth*[120]

But what followed was also, once, an effort to crawl
toward me made by my bundled-up little larva that had
been laid down for a moment on my bed. What
animal perfection! The little creature guessed, she
sensed the presence of my forbidden milk, and
blindly struggled toward that blocked source. Never
did I cry more brokenheartedly. Dreadful it is to ask
in vain, but small is that hurt when compared with
the pain of not giving. . . .

From Colette's autobiography[121]

THE WIPING MOSS FROM THE RUINS

Running to me—
My wiping moss—
Breakneck from the ruined house.

Well, a nipple full of milk
And a fine pot-stone, yes,
Welcome as the light of spring,
Welcome as a seal in spring!

Well, the milk of the nipple, listen,
Listen: hear them shout
Where is that milk?
All the way up from Ipsetaleq.

An Eskimo song[122]

But I lying the next chamber to her and did hear
her, when she came out of them, to give great shrieks
and suddenly, that it frightened me extremely, and all
the time of this poor child's illness I myself was at
death's door by the extreme excess of those, upon
the fright and terror came upon me, so great floods
that I was spent, and my breath lost, my strength
departed from me, and I could not speak for faintings,
and dispirited so that my dear mother and aunt and
friends did not expect my life, but overcome with
sorrow for me. Nor durst they tell me in what a
condition my dear Naly was in her fits, lest grief for
her, added to my own extremity, with loss of blood,
might have extinguished my miserable life: but
removing her in her cradle into the Blue Parlor, a
great way off me, lest I hearing her sad shrieks should
renew my sorrows. These extremities did so lessen
my milk, that though I began to recruit strength, yet
I must be subject to the changes of my condition.
After my dear Naly was in most miraculous mercy
restored to me the next day, and recruited my strength;
within a fortnight I recovered my milk, and was
overjoyed to give my sweet Betty suck, which I did,
and began to recover to a miracle, blessed be my
great and gracious Lord God, Who remembered
mercy towards me.

From the diary of Alice Thornton, January 1654[123]

PRIVATE ENTRY IN THE DIARY
OF A FEMALE PARENT

He is my own fault. Let me see it straight.
I got him willfully, with joy, and hatched him
a long time intimately, and in him warmed
the flaws and fineness of two ancestries,
before I had my bellyful of him
at last and threw him neck and crop
into the doctor's expert rubber hands.
Since then I've suckled, kissed and smacked him
while he has sucked and wet and beaten me
or all but beaten me, although I rise
out of the ashes at short intervals.
The end will be, perhaps, the end of me,
which will, I humbly guess, be his beginning

By Dilys Laing[124]

Chapter
Seven

Motherhood

Sleep, darling

I have a small
daughter called
Cleis, who is

like a golden
flower
        I wouldn't
take all Croesus'
kingdom with love
thrown in, for her

By Sappho[125]

    My dear Love—I began to wish so earnestly to hear
from you, that the sight of your letters occasioned
such pleasurable emotions, I was obliged to throw them
aside till the little girl and I were alone together;
and this said little girl, our darling, is become a most
intelligent little creature, and as gay as a lark, and that
in the morning too, which I do not find quite so
convenient. I once told you, that the sensations before
she was born, and when she is sucking, were pleasant;
but they do not deserve to be compared to the emotions
I feel, when she stops to smile upon me, or laughs
outright on meeting me unexpectedly in the street,
or after a short absence. She has now the advantage
of having two good nurses, and I am at present able
to discharge my duty to her, without being the slave
of it.

From the letters of Mary Wollstonecraft,
dated October 26, 1794[126]

LETTER TO MY CHILDREN

I guided you by rote—
Nipple to spoon, from spoon
To knife and fork,
And many a weak maternal morning
Bored the breakfast hour
With 'manners make the man',
And cleanliness I kissed
But shunned its neighbour,
Puzzled all my days
By the 'I' in godliness.

Before you turn
And bare your faultless teeth at me
Accept a useless gift, apology,
Admit I churched you in the rites
Of trivia
And burned the family incense
At a false god's altar.

If we could start again,
You, newbegotten, I
A clean stick peeled
Of twenty paper layers of years
I'd tell you only what you know
But barely know you know,
Teach one commandment,
'Mind the senses and the soul
Will take care of itself,
Being five times blessed.'

By Anne Wilkinson[127]

So in the villages there was a year of hunger.
That year, Jabavu's elder sister, three years old, came
running playfully to her mother's teats, and found
herself smacked off, like a troublesome puppy. The
mother was still feeding Jabavu, who had always been
a demanding, hungry child, and there was a new baby
a month old. The winter was cold and dusty. The men
went hunting for hares and buck, the women
searched through the bush all day for greens and
roots, and there was hardly any grain for the porridge.
The dust filled the villages, the dust hung in sullen
clouds in the air, blew into the huts and into the
nostrils of the people. The little girl died—it was sad
because she had breathed too much dust. And the
mother's breasts hung limp, and when Jabavu came
tugging at her dress she smacked him off. She was
sick with grief because of the death of the child, and
also with fear for the baby. For now the buck and
hares were scarce, they had been hunted so
relentlessly, and one cannot keep life on leaves and
roots. But Jabavu did not relinquish his mother's
breasts so easily. At night, as she lay on her mat, the
new baby beside her, Jabavu came pushing and
struggling to her milk, and she woke, startled, saying:
'Ehhh, but this child of mine is strong.' He was only
a year old, yet she had to use all her strength to fend
him off. In the dark of the hut her husband woke and
lifted Jabavu, screaming and kicking, away from
her, and away from the tender new baby. That baby
died, but by then Jabavu had turned sullen and was
fighting like a little leopard for what scraps of food
there were. A little skeleton he was, with loose brown
skin and enormous, frantic eyes, nosing around in the
dust for fallen mealies or a scrap of sour vegetable.

This is what the mother thinks of, as she crouches
watching the wisps of steam curl off the water. For

her Jabavu is three children, she loves him still with
all the bereaved passion of that terrible year. She
thinks: It was then, when he was so tiny, that Jabavu
the Big Mouth was made—yes, the people called him
the Big Mouth even then. Yes, it is the fault of the
Long Hunger that Jabavu is as he is.

From Hunger, *by Doris Lessing*[128]

My little son
Where have they hidden you?
My little son
Have they put you behind the grain-bin?
Have they hidden you down in the wheat-field?
Have they taken you to the forest
And covered you with leaves?
O where have they hidden you
My little son?

An Indian folksong: mother's mourning
sung for her son[129]

Every year Sophie had a new baby. Almost every
year she buried one. Her little graves were dotted
all over the cemetery. I never knew more than three
of her twenty-one children to be alive at one time.
By the time she was in her early fifties every child
was dead and Sophie had cried her eyes dry. Then she
took to drink.

From Klee Wyck, *by Canadian painter*
and writer Emily Carr[130]

THE LULLABY OF THE SNOW

Cold, cold this night is my bed,
Cold, cold this night is my child,
Lasting, lasting this night thy sleep,
I in my shroud and thou in mine arm.

Over me creeps the shadow of death,
The warm pulse of my love will not stir,
The wind of the heights thy sleep-lulling,
The close-clinging snow of the peaks thy mantle.

Over thee creeps the hue of death,
White angels are floating in the air,
The Son of grace each season guards thee,
The Son of my God keeps the watch with me.

Though loud my cry my plaint is idle,
Though sore my struggle no friend shares it;
Thy body-shirt is the snow of the peaks,
Thy death-bed the fen of the valleys.

Thine eye is closed, thy sleep is heavy,
Thy mouth to my breast, but thou seekest no milk;
My croon of love thou shalt never know,
My plaint of love thou shalt never tell.

A cold arm-burden my love on my bosom,
A frozen arm-burden without life or breath;
May the angels of God make smooth the road,
May the angels of God be calling us home.

A hard frost no thaw shall subdue,
The frost of the grave which no spring shall make green,
A lasting sleep which morn shall not break,
The death-slumber of mother and child.

Heavenly light directs my feet,
The music of the skies gives peace to my soul,
Alone I am under the wing of the Rock,
Angels of God calling me home.

Cold, cold, cold is my child,
Cold, cold is the mother who watches thee,
Sad, sad, sad is my plaint,
As the tinge of death creeps over me.

O Cross of the heavens, sign my soul,
O Mother of breastlings, shield my child,
O Son of tears whom a mother nurtured,
Show thy tenderness in death to the needy.

A dying woman's song, from the Highlands
of Scotland[131]

It is time that my mother comes home!
It is dark outside.
Darkness has fallen upon the earth.
When it is dark, and the sun is near to set,
When the jackal comes out from the bush
And you hear him shout out loud,
The hyena hearing the howl,
Comes out suddenly leaving the forest,
While the master-hyena looks around stealthily,
Saying "If only I could find somewhere
    a dead animal . . .
Only a dead animal?
Oh no!

If the hyena gets (hold of) a person,
He will never let him go.
When does a hyena let go of a person
Who is (found) alone and tired?
With whom will our mother return?
Darkness has fallen, it will be all dark.
Perhaps the hyena is waiting for her on the road . . .

An Ethiopian lullaby[132]

THE LOST BABY POEM

the time i dropped your almost body down
down to meet the waters under the city
and run one with the sewage to the sea
what did i know about waters rushing back
what did i know about drowning
or being drowned

you would have been born into winter
in the year of the disconnected gas
and no car   we would have made the thin
walk of Genesee Hill into Canada wind
to watch you slip like ice into strangers' hands
you would have fallen naked as snow into winter
if you were here i could tell you these
and some other things

if i am ever less than a mountain
for your definite brothers and sisters
let the rivers pour over my head
let the sea take me for a spiller
of seas   let black men call me stranger
always   for your never named sake

By the modern poet Lucille Clifton[133]

THE MOTHER

Abortions will not let you forget.
You remember the children you got that you did not get,
The damp small pulps with a little or with no hair,
The singers and workers that never handled the air.
You will never neglect or beat
Them, or silence or buy with a sweet.
You will never wind up the sucking-thumb
Or scuttle off ghosts that come.
You will never leave them, controlling your luscious sigh,
Return for a snack of them, with gobbling mother-eye.

I have heard in the voices of the wind the voices of my
    dim killed children
I have contracted. I have eased
My dim dears at the breasts they could never suck.
I have said, Sweets, if I sinned, if I seized
Your luck
And your lives from your unfinished reach,
If I stole your births and your names,
Your straight baby tears and your games,
Your stilted or lovely loves, your tumults, your
    marriages, aches, and your deaths,
If I poisoned the beginnings of your breaths,
Believe that even in my deliberateness I was not
    deliberate.
Though why should I whine,
Whine that the crime was other than mine? —
Since anyhow you are dead.
Or rather, or instead,
You were never made.
But that too, I am afraid,
Is faulty: oh, what shall I say, how is the truth to be said?
You were born, you had body, you died.

It is just that you never giggled or planned or cried.
Believe me, I loved you all.
Believe me, I knew you, though faintly, and I loved,
    I loved you
All.

By *Gwendolyn Brooks*[134]

PARENTHOOD

My child is like a stone
in wilderness
pick it up and rub it on the cheek
there's no response
or toss it down . . .
only a hollow sound
but hold it in the hand
a little time
it warms, it curves
softly into the palm:
even a stone takes on a pulse
in a warm hold

By *Dorothy Livesay*[135]

I have the queerest feelings of having been reborn
with Frieda—it's as if my real, rich, happy life only
started just about then. I suppose it's a case of
knowing what one wants. I never really knew before.
I hope I shall always be a 'young' mother like you. I
think working or having any sort of career keeps one
young longer. I feel I'm just beginning at writing, too.
Doing prose is much easier on me; the concentration
spreads out over a large area and doesn't stand or
fall on one day's work, like a poem.

. . . Well, I must get supper for my family. Lots of
love from us all.

Sylvia Plath's letter to her mother[136]

When it is the first born child of the one who has
just for the first time given birth, a young woman,
then the woman is really fond of her child. Then she
engages a carver to make a little canoe and all kinds
of playthings for the boy. And if it is a girl, then
she engages a doll maker to make dolls of alder wood,
and women are hired by her to make little mats and
little dishes and little spoons and all kinds of things of
this kind, even if the child of the woman may be only
five months old. Then her child begins to get sick,
and not long is sick the child when it dies and the
woman carries in her arms her child. Then all the
relatives of the woman come to see her and all the
women wail together. As soon as all the women stop
crying the mother of the child speaks aloud. she says,

"Ah, ah, ah, what is the reason, child, that you
have done this to me? I have tried hard to treat you
well when you came to me to have me for your

mother. Look at all your toys and all the kinds of
things. What is the reason that you desert me, child?
May it be that I did something, child, to you in the
way I treated you, child? I will try better when you
come back to me, child. Please, only become at once
well in the place to which you are going. As soon as
you are made well, please, come back to me, child.
Please, do not stay away there. Please, only have
mercy on me who is your mother, child," says she.
Then they put the child in the coffin and they put it
up on a hemlock tree. That is the end.

A Kwakiutl Indian prayer of a Mother
for her dead child[137]

A JOYFUL MOTHER OF CHILDREN

Of children nine and twenty that I bore,
Nor son nor daughter but remains alive:
No staff mine aged hand hath trembled o'er:
I ended well my fivescore years and five.

An ancient Greek poem[138]

Young men there are in plenty,
   But I love only one;
Him I've not seen for long,
   Though he is my only son.
When he comes, I'll haste to meet him,
   I think of him all night;
He too will be glad to see me,
   His eyes will gleam with delight.

The song of a Kioway Indian mother
whose son has gone to war[139]

He who was wont to give me beautiful things, the
    son of Noworb,
He is dead.
Arise. Why do you lie there?
Do what your companions do, go and play.
Son of my beloved, why do you lie there?
Arise, run and play, that I may see you.
Your companions go away from you.
Whom shall I now send to fetch water?
Whom have you left behind for me?
Son of Gakhubes, arise that I may carry you on
    my back.

     A North African song on the death of a child[40]

Clinging to my neck, the children cried out,
And asked where Mother was going:
"We hear you'll be leaving us soon,
But when will you come back again?
Our mother has always been kind,
Why should she be cruel to us now?
We are so young, so little.
How can you bear to leave us behind?"

Seeing this, I felt my body collapsed,
My spirit shattered, my mind crazed.
Caressing my children, I wept, I wailed.
Again and again I turned to gaze at them.

Many others had been captured with me
And some came to bid me goodbye,
Envious that I alone could go home.
Their wails and laments wrung my heart.
For the moment the horses stood still;

The chariot wheels would not turn around:
The spectators sobbed as they watched,
Even passers-by wept at our departure.

Gone, gone! cut off from loved ones,
I hurried homeward on my long journey.
Three thousand leagues separating us,
Could we hope to see each other again?
I thought of the children I had borne,
My heart felt as if stabbed.

Home, I found my family all gone;
Not even cousins had survived.
City walls turned to woody mounds,
Courtyards overgrown with thorns and brambles.
Bleak bones knew not to whom they belonged:
Unburied, uncovered, scattered far and wide.

Outside the door, I heard no human voice,
Only howling and barking wolves.
All alone, I gazed at my shadow.
Fear seized me and robbed me of all my senses.

Climbing a mound, I looked into the distance.
My soul seemed to have left my body;
I left as if my life had ended.
But bystanders revived and comforted me,
Only then did I force myself to live on.

By the Chinese poet Ts'ai Yen, c. A.D. 200[141]

MATERNAL GRIEF

I am not human,
I am not human,
Nor am I divine.

To whom,
to whom can I cry,
'I am thine'?

I have picked my grandsire's corpse to the bone,
I have found no ghost in brisket or chine.
I have shed the blood of my female kin,
but they never return to speak again.

I am not human,
I am not human,
How shall I feed my hungry children?

I make the porridge of meal and wine
and pour it out in the troughs for swine.

The ghosts are hungry, the ghosts are divine,
but the pigs eat the meal, and the priests drink the wine.

By Kathleen Raine (1908—)[142]

The bird that saw sings
Tseutse's child is dead
She should eat, they say
I don't want to eat, she says
God himself greeted them
And said, she should eat
But Tseutse refused and said:
I'll never eat

Then earth greeted them
and said she should eat
But Tseutse said never will I eat
Foufou she desired
but said to eat she doesn't want
the mush was her envy
but said to eat she wouldn't want
But nevertheless stole the ripe fruit and ate them

A song from Ghana[143]

TO A CHILD BORN IN
TIME OF SMALL WAR

Child, you were conceived in my upstairs room,
my girlhood all around. Later I spent
nights there alone imploring the traitor moon
to keep me childless still. I never meant
to bear you in this year of discontent.

Yet you were there in your appointed place,
remnant of leaving, of a sacrament.
Child, if I loved you then, it was to trace
on a cold sheet your likeness to his absent face.

In May we were still alone. That month your life
stirred in my dark, as if my body's core
grew quick with wings. I turned away, more wife
than mother still, unwilling to explore
the fact of you. There was an orient shore,
a tide of hurt, that held my heart and mind.
It was as if you lived behind a door
I was afraid to open, lest you bind
my breaking. Lost in loss, I was not yours to find.

I swelled with summer. You were hard and strong,
making me know you were there. When the mail
brought me no letter, and the time was long
between the war's slow gains, and love seemed frail,
I fought you. You were error, judgment, jail.
Without you, there were ways I, too, could fight
a war. Trapped in your growing, I would rail
against your grotesque carriage, swollen, tight.
I would have left you, and I did in dreams of flight.

Discipline of the seasons brought me round.
Earth comes to term and so, in time, did we.
You are a living thing of sight and sound.
Nothing of you is his, you are all of me:
your sex, gray eye, the struggle to be free
that made your birth like death, but I awake
for that caught air, your cry. I try to see,
but cannot, the same lift his eyebrows take.
Child, if I love you now, it is for your own sake.

The contemporary poet Helen Sorrells[144]

Ejaja-eja.
A bit of song comes back.
I draw it to me like a friend.
   Ejaja-eja.

I ought, I suppose, to be ashamed
of the child I once carried on my back,
when I heard he'd left the settlement.
They're right to tell me so:
I ought to be ashamed.
   Ejaja-eja.

I am ashamed:
because he didn't have a mother
who was faultless
as the clear sky,
wise and without folly.
Now that he's the butt
of everybody's tongue,
this evil talk will finish him.
   Ejaja-eja.

He has become the burden
of my age.
But far from being
properly ashamed,
I'm envious of others
when they break up
after feasts, and set off
with crowds of friends
behind them, waving on the ice.
   Ejaja-eja.

I remember one mild spring.
We'd camped near Cross-Eye Lake.
Our footsteps sank

with a soft creak
into half-thawed snow.

I stayed near the men,
like a tame animal.
But when the news
about the murder came,
and that he'd fled,
the ground heaved under me
like a mountain,
and I stood on its summit,
and I staggered.

*The song of an Eskimo mother whose son
has murdered his companion*[145]

PARADIGM

Through the summer windows of afternoon
sunslanted, an old woman
stout and ungainly who lugs
jars of pickled herring to the least
grateful of daughters-in-law
calls suddenly
Jane!
in a young girl's voice to the youngest
I see you, Jane!
tottering granddaughter, piercing other
echoes of the girl
running the dusty streets of a Polish village
I catch you!
fifty years ago.

Sometimes on a country porch
a gap-toothed crone in a checkered kerchief holding
a toothless child high between twisted hands
utters a nameless necessary battle-cry.

I see my children have all my proud faults
no changelings: endless
red ribbons braided
into the child's blood go skimming
unfathomable steps of light.

By the contemporary Canadian poet
Phyllis Gotlieb[146]

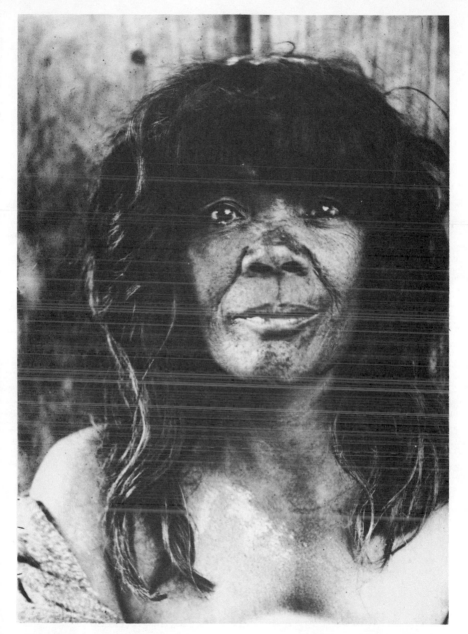

Chapter
Eight

The Changing
Seasons

SISTERS

Can I easily say,
I know you of course now,
no longer the fellow-victim,
reader of my diaries, heir
to my outgrown dresses,
ear for my poems and invectives?
Do I know you better
than that blue-eyed stranger
self-absorbed as myself
raptly knitting or sleeping
through a thirdclass winter journey?
Face to face all night
her dreams and whimpers
tangled with mine,
sleeping but not asleep
behind the engine drilling
into dark Germany,
her eyes, mouth, head
reconstructed by dawn
as we nodded farewell.
Her I should recognize
years later, anywhere.

By the contemporary poet Adrienne Rich[147]

WOMEN

My three sisters are sitting
on rocks of black obsidian.
For the first time, in this light, I can see who they are.

My first sister is sewing her costume for the procession.

She is going as the Transparent Lady
and all her nerves will be visible.

My second sister is also sewing,
at the seam over her heart which has never healed entirely.
At last, she hopes, this tightness in her chest will ease.

My third sister is gazing.
at a dark-red crust spreading westward far out on the sea.
Her stockings are torn but she is beautiful.

By Adrienne Rich[148]

A WOMAN MOURNED BY DAUGHTERS

Now, not a tear begun,
we sit here in your kitchen,
spent, you see, already.
You are swollen till you strain
this house and the whole sky.
You, whom we so often
succeeded in ignoring!
You are puffed up in death
like a corpse pulled from the sea;
we groan beneath your weight.
And yet you were a leaf,
a straw blown on the bed,
you had long since become
crisp as a dead insect.
What is it, if not you,
that settles on us now
like satin you pulled down
over our bridal heads?
What rises in our throats
like food you prodded in?

Nothing could be enough.
You breathe upon us now
through solid assertions
of yourself: teaspoons, goblets,
seas of carpet, a forest
of old plants to be watered,
an old man in an adjoining
room to be touched and fed.
And all this universe
dares us to lay a finger
anywhere, save exactly
as you would wish it done.

By Adrienne Rich[149]

What happy days they were when father came!
For me, who lived within the garden all the year,
it was just a plain great garden; but when he came
it was transformed. It became a place of rare enchant-
ment, with fairy palaces and lakes of jewelled water,
and the lotus flowers took on a loveliness for which
there is no name. We would sit hand-in-hand in our
gaily painted tea-house, and watch the growing of the
lotus from the first unfurling of the leaf to the fall
of the dying flower. When it rained, we would see the
leaves raise their eager, dark-green cups until filled,
then bend down gracefully to empty their fulness,
and rise to catch the drops again . . .

My father loved the silence, and taught me that
it is in the silence, in the quiet places, rather than
on the housetops, that one can hear the spirit's call,
and forget the clanging of the world.

A traditional Chinese lady's reflections[150]

Alas, alas, O Goddess, what misfortune has brought
    me here?
Standing in the field Banelin weeps.
At home mother-in-law torments me,
At home my sisters-in-law abuse me,
In the jungle my husband bullies me.
Alas, alas, O Goddess.
For twelve years have I cleared away the cow-dung,
But mother-in-law is never pleased,
Sister-in-law is never pleased,
Husband is never pleased.
They snatch the dung out of my hands
And beat me with it.
Standing in the field Banelin weeps.
For twelve years I have swept the yard,
But they snatch the broom out of my hands
And beat me with it.
For twelve years I have brought water for the house
But they snatch away my gundri
And beat me with it.
Standing in the field Banelin weeps.

An Indian folksong: the unhappy
relationships of woman[151]

ON THE DEATH OF ANNE BRONTE

There's little joy in life for me,
    And little terror in the grave;
I've lived the parting hour to see
    Of one I would have died to save.

Calmly to watch the failing breath,
    Wishing each sigh might be the last;
Longing to see the shade of death
    O'er those beloved features cast;

The cloud, the stillness that must part
    The darling of my life from me;
And then to thank God from my heart,
    To thank him well and fervently;

Although I knew that we had lost
    The hope and glory of our life;
And now, benighted, tempest-tossed,
    Must bear alone the weary strife.

By Charlotte Brontë[152]

AFTER GRIEF

Death halves us:
every loss
divides
our narrowness
and we are less.

But more:
each losing's an encore
of clapping hands
dreaming us on;
the same scene played once more
willing us grander than
we were:
no dwarf 'menines'
but kings and queens.

And still, some say
death raises up
gathers the soul strong-limbed
above the common tide

to catch a glimpse
(over world's wailing wall)
of an exultant countryside.

By Dorothy Livesay[153]

THE GRANDMOTHERS

They moved like rivers in their mended stockings,
Their skirts, their buns, their bodies grown
Round as trees. Over the kitchen fires
They hoarded magics, and the heavy bowls
Of Sunday bread rose up faithful as light.
We smiled for them, although they never spoke.
Silent as stones, they merely stared when birds
Fell in the leaves, or brooms wore out, or children
Scraped their knees and cried. Within my village,
We did not think it odd or ask for words;
In their vast arms we knew that we were loved.
I remember their happiness at the birth of children.
I remember their hands, swollen and hard as wood;
And how sometimes in summer when the night
Was thick with stars, they gathered in the garden.
Near sleep, I watched them as they poured the wine,
Hung paper lanterns in the alien birches.
Then one would take a tiny concertina
And cradle it against her mammoth apron,
Till music hung like ribbons in the trees
And round my bed. Oh, still within my dreams,
Softly they gather under summer stars
And sing of the far Danube, of Vienna,
Clear as a flight of wild and slender girls!

By the contemporary poet Mary Oliver[154]

GRANDMOTHER

O lovely raw red wild
autumn turning
it's time to think of the blood
the red searing

Pale pale the poets and poetasters
moving along the midnight mists
those riverbanks where girls
white flanked, never refuse
yield all their mysteries

Give me instead
a small child noting
holly and rowan berry ripen
a small hand clasped

Who's there? What's that?
O, to survive
what must we do
to believe?
In the trees, my grandson.
In these roots. In these leaves.

By Dorothy Livesay[155]

"The other day I asked her how she can be in such
good spirits; she has bad arthritis, and her digestion
is not of the best. 'My sister,' she said, 'my life is not
mine; it belongs to God. I am afraid to die. I do not
want to die. I cannot persuade myself to like being
old.I am no magician who can make a trance for
herself, and end up welcoming what is a fearful

moment: the last breath. But I have been given ten
years short of a century already, and I don't seem to
be leaving yet, for all my aches and pains. I am
rich with years, a millionaire! I have been part of
my own generation, then I watched my children's
generation grow up, then my grandchildren's, and now
my great-grandchildren's. Two of my great-grandchildren are becoming full-grown women now; they
come visit me, and will remember me. Now, I ask
you, how much more can a woman expect? My
great-granddaughter told her teacher I was a barber
fifty years ago, and the teacher wanted to send my
name to Santa Fe, and they would honor me as a
pioneer among women. Well, imagine that! I said no.
I have been honored already—all this life I've been
given is an honor God has chosen to offer. It is a big
achievement, if I say so myself, to have accumulated
all these years. And as I look back and think, I decide
that I wouldn't have done things any different, not for
the most part, anyway.'

   "I am taking liberties with what she said, but I
can remember her words, because my head tries hard
to hold on to almost every one of them. I told my
husband her message, and he nodded. I thought:
It will not stay with him, he only keeps the old
memories. But yesterday he said she is a wise woman,
my sister—for two days he had been thinking of her
speech to me. 'Do you think we should be proud,
even if we have a few more years until we're her age?'
he asked me. I didn't answer him. He didn't need an
answer. I hugged him—oh, I was ashamed for a
second, because my son walked in, and so did a
customer. 'So, that's how you two mind the store for
me,' our son said. And the customer, she was a young
woman carrying her first child, and she said she had

something to dream about now: if only she and her
husband could live so long and still feel love for
each other."

The words of an old woman of New Mexico[156]

WASHING AND POUNDING CLOTHES

I know that you will not come back from war.
    Still, on this stone
I pound your cloak while you must die afar
    And I alone.

Here in this bitter autumn chill I dream
    You may be warm
Although the heart's chill that I suffer seems
    An equal harm.

How can I cease from toiling, since I pray
    This coat may come
To the Great Wall you guard, while I must stay
    In our cold home?

Each sinew in my woman's body pounds
    Your garment fair:
Listen! You may even hear these sounds
    Out there!

By Tu Fu[157]

WIDOW

No longer any man needs me
nor is the dark night of love
coupled

But the body is relentless, knows
its need
must satisfy itself without the seed
must shake in dreams, fly up the stairs
backwards.

In the open box in the attic
a head lies, set sideways.

This head from this body is severed.

By Dorothy Livesay[158]

THE LAMENTATIONS

Of their lament white-armed Andromache
Was leader, holding in her hands the while
The head of slaughterous Hector: 'O my man,
Thou art gone young from life, and leavest me
A widow in thy house! Thy son is yet
Only a babe, whom we two luckless ones
Begot; nor can I hope for him to come
To manhood, for ere that this city must
Be wasted root and branch. For thou art gone,
Who didst watch over it and keep it safe
And guard its noble wives and little ones.
And they will doubtless soon go riding on
The hollow ships, and I along with them;
And thither thou, my child, wilt follow me,

Where thou wilt labour at unseemly tasks,
Toiling before a brutal master's eyes;
Or else some Greek will seize thee by the arm
And hurl thee from the wall, a ghastly death,
Some rancorous man whose brother Hector killed
Or else his son or father, since full many
Achaeans bit vast earth at Hector's hands;
For in distressful war thy father's touch
Was not caressing: therefore through the city
The people mourn him. Hector, grief untold
and desolation hast thou brought thy parents;
But the extremity of sorrow will
Be left to me, for in thy death thou didst not
Stretch out thy hands towards me from thy bed,
Nor speak to me one pregnant word, whereon
I might have wept and pondered night and day.'

    And so she mourned; the women joined her wail.
Then Hecuba took up the throbbing dirge:
'Hector, of all my sons the best beloved,
Thou in thy life wert dear unto the gods,
And even in the doom of death they have
Shown care for thee. For other sons of mine
Swift-foot Achilles, when he took them, sold
Across the sterile sea to Samos' isle,
Imbros, or Lemnos hid in steam. But when
He took thy life with the long bladed bronze,
He dragged thee many a time around the barrow
Of his own friend Patroclus, whom thou slewest;
Yet for all that he could not raise him up.
And now I see thee lying here at home
All dewy fresh, new-slain, like some one whom
Apollo of the silver bow hath reached
With painless darts and killed.'

    And so she mourned and stirred the hopeless wail
Once more. But third to lead the dirge for them

Was Helen: 'Hector, whom I loved the best
Of all my husband's brothers; being the wife
of godlike Alexander, him, who brought me
To Troy—and would that I had died ere that!'

By Homer[159]

When a person has died the men bring their little drums.
Mothers of Monga yo yo pray for Monga
War has crushed him how did war crush him?
Cry my gullet, mother of Monga yo yo pray for Monga
War has crushed him O how did war crush him?
When they have finished crying they dance and sing
　　all day long.

A mourning song of the Ba-Totela of Zaire[160]

THE WEAVER'S LAMENTATION

You have left me to linger in hopeless longing,
Your presence had ever made me feel no want,
You have left me to travel in sorrow.
Left me to travel in sorrow; Ah! the pain,
Left me to travel in sorrow; Ah! the pain, the pain,
　　the pain.

You have left me to linger in hopeless longing,
In your presence there was no sorrow,
You have gone and sorrow I shall feel, as I travel,
　　Ah! the pain, the pain.

You have gone and sorrow I shall feel as I travel,
You have left me in hopeless longing.

In your presence there was no sorrow,
You have gone and sorrow I shall feel as I travel;
   Ah! the pain, the pain, the pain.

Content with your presence, I wanted nothing more,
You have left me to travel in sorrow; Ah! the pain,
   the pain, the pain!

> *A lamentation for her dead relatives, sung by the*
> *weaver in the Osage tribe of American Indians* [161]

THE LAST YEARS

Now that my loves are dead
On what shall my action ride?

I will not make my children
Lovers nor tune my time
By footsteps of the young
To ease my solitude;

But sing of springs, forgotten
In slow summer's tedium,
And autumn ripe with fruit;
Of winter branches, bare

Beneath the storm, bowed
With weight of rain, and after,
Lifting knotted fingers
Towards a translucent sky;

And wrest from the gathered sheaf
Forgiveness, buried in the heart
Of every grain, to knead
My bread for sustenance.

My action, sharing bread,
Love becomes ability
To bless, and be, in blessing,
Blessed.

By the contemporary writer
Irene Claremont de Castillejo[162]

"Look at him oh, do look at him, Minet-Cheri!
Goodness! Isn't he funny!"

And she laughed, sitting there in her mourning,
laughed her shrill, young girl's laugh, clapping her
hands with delight at the kitten. Then, of a sudden,
searing memory stemmed that brilliant cascade and
dried the tears of laughter in my mother's eyes. Yet
she offered no excuse for having laughed, either on
that day or on the days that followed: for though she
had lost the man she passionately loved, in her
kindness for us she remained among us just as she
always had been, accepting her sorrow as she would
have accepted the advent of a long and dreary
season, but welcoming from every source the fleeting
benediction of joy. So she lived on, swept by shadow
and sunshine, bowed by bodily torments, resigned,
unpredictable and generous, rich in children, flowers,
and animals like a fruitful domain.

Colette's memories of her mother[163]

White Painted Woman has reached middle age by
     means of it,
  She has reached middle age by means of it,
  By means of it she has entered long life,
  She has reached middle age by means of it.

He made the black staff of old age for me,
He made the road of the sun for me;
These holy things he has made for me, saying,
"With these you will grow old."
Now when I have become old,
You will remember me by means of them.

An Apache commemoration of middle age
and old age[164]

RONDEL

Now that I am fifty-six
Come and celebrate with me—

What happens to song and sex
Now that I am fifty-six?

They dance, but differently,
Death and distance in the mix;
Now that I am fifty-six
Come and celebrate with me.

By Muriel Rukeyser[165]

She is very beautiful
But her young breasts are fallen
He fondles them no longer
That once were his loved playthings
Youth passes quickly, quickly
But a girl's youth endures
The shortest time of all.

A folksong of India[166]

CLARINDA'S INDIFFERENCE AT
PARTING WITH HER BEAUTY

Now, age came on, and all the dismal traine
That fright the vitious, and afflicte the vaine.
Departing beauty, now Clarinda spies
Pale in her cheeks, and dying in her eyes;
That youthfull air, that wanders ore the face,
That undescrib'd, that unresisted grace,
Those morning beams, that strongly warm, and shine,
Which men that feel and see, can ne're define,
Now, on the wings of restlesse time, were fled,
And ev'ning shades, began to rise, and spread,
When thus resolv'd, and ready soon to part,
Slighting the short repreives of proffer'd art
She spake—
And what, vain beauty, didst thou'ere atchieve,
When at thy height, that I thy fall shou'd greive,
When, did'st thou e're successfully persue?
When, did'st thou e're th'appointed foe subdue?
'Tis vain of numbers, or of strength to boast,
In an undisciplin'd, unguided Host,
And love, that did thy mighty hopes deride,
Wou'd pay no sacrafice, but to thy pride.
When, did'st thou e're a pleasing rule obtain,
A glorious Empire's but a glorious pain,
Thou, art indeed, but vanity's cheife sourse,
But foyle to witt, to want of witt a curse,
For often, by thy gaudy sign's descry'd
A fool, which unobserv'd, had been untry'd,
And when thou doest such empty things adorn,
'Tis but to make them more the publick scorn.
I know thee well, but weak thy reign wou'd be
Did n'one adore, or prize thee more then me.
I see indeed, thy certain ruine neer,
But can't affoard one parting sigh, or tear,

Nor rail at Time, nor quarrell with my glasse,
But unconcern'd, can lett thy glories passe.

*"Clarinda's Indifference at Parting with
Her Beauty," by Anne Finch (1623–1673)*[167]

BREATHING

"You smell good
    you smell
as a woman should"

There have been eaters
    and drinkers of me
    painters of me
    eye bright
    and one singer
    who wreathed me
    in an aria

But I had yet to discover
    how ever in old age
    a woman moves
    with freshness
is a leaf   perhaps
or a breath of wind
in a man's nostrils

By Dorothy Livesay[168]

Alas, I draw breath heavily,
my lungs breathe heavily,
as I call for my song.

When the news arrived
of far-off friends,
starving for winter game,
I wanted to sing:
to invoke the words from above,
the music from above.
Hajaja!

I forget the fire in my chest,
and the wheeze of the lungs
while I sing,
and I remember the old times
when I was strong.

These were times
when no-one rivalled me
at flensing seal;
when all alone, I boned and cut
the lean flesh
of three great reindeer-bulls
for drying!

Look: delicious slices
spread out on the mountain-stones
while the sun rides up the sky
in the cool morning,
in the cool morning!

An old woman's song, from the Caribou Eskimos[169]

AGING

My body haunts me
thieves in on me at night
shattering sleep
with nameless pointless pains

Where do you ache?
The Chinese doctor's skill
might poise with needle
over my tossing form

but there's no
one still spot   no
one still time I'd swear:
The pain is here.

And every night
my fingers search the wound, the old
spine curvature the creaking knees . . .
but tongues, the darting tongues
lick elsewhere, fan desire
until all yesterdays are gulfed
in freezing fire.

By Dorothy Livesay[170]

SONG OF THE OLD WOMAN

all these heads these ears these eyes
around me
how long will the ears hear me?
and those eyes how long
will they look at me?
when these ears won't hear me any more
when these eyes turn aside from my eyes
I'll eat no more raw liver with fat
and those eyes won't see me any more
and my hair my hair will have disappeared

From the Netsilik Eskimos[171]

Old age has come, my head is shaking
Sitting on a stool my mind repents too late
I have no mother now, no brother and no family
No one will take me into their home
Sitting on a stool I think
Too late, I think again
Life has become sorrow
More than can be borne
O earth, break open and take me in.
In my parents' kingdom
I played and danced
But in my own kingdom there is sorrow
O earth, break open and take me in

A folksong of India[172]

A baby nurse is one that changes diapers and loves
'em dearly. Get up at all hours of the night to give 'em
the bottle and change their pants. If the baby coughs
or cries, you have to find out the need. I had my
own room usually, but I slept in the same room with
the baby. I would take full charge. It was twenty-four
hours. I used to have one day a week off and I'd go home
and see my own two little ones. It's been so long I've
almost forgotten what I was.

Babies are rewarding. No matter what, they cry
all night. I like 'em. I go baby-sitting for those that
need me, two-, three-, five-year-olds. I even baby-sat
last week.

I'm never gonna retire. What for? As long as I can
be useful and needed someplace, I'll work. Even if I
can't scrub floors, I'll do some other things. When
that day comes when I can't work, I'll be a lost soul.

An old woman remembers[173]

STANZAS

I'll not weep that thou art going to leave me,
  There's nothing lovely here;
And doubly will the dark world grieve me,
  While thy heart suffers there.

I'll not weep, because the summer's glory
  Must always end in gloom;
And, follow out the happiest story—
  It closes with a tomb!

And I am weary of the anguish
  Increasing winters bear;
Weary to watch the spirit languish
  Through years of dead despair.

So, if a tear, when thou art dying,
  Should haply fall from me,
It is but that my soul is sighing,
  To go and rest with thee.

By Emily Brontë[174]

Long ago, the Indians were traveling. And some old woman was among them. And it seems they did not like her.

Then it seems they spoke thus: "This old woman is good for nothing," they said. Then they had spoken thus. "This old woman is good for nothing," they said; "therefore, let's abandon her," they said. Then they had abandoned her.

Then it seems she wept. Then these Mountain Spirits came to her. And they spoke thus to her: "Why are you weeping?" they said to her.

"I weep because they have abandoned me," she said. "I cannot see, I cannot hear, and I cannot speak. For that reason, I weep."

Then they began to sing for her. And she who had been blind, her eyes were made to open. She who had been deaf began to hear again. She who had been blind was made to see again.

Then they spoke thus to her: "This that we have done is good. When you return, tell them about it," they said to her.

Then she performed all of the ceremony they had done for her in exactly their way. And in that way she returned.

Then she performed all of that which had been given to her in exactly their way. And, in this way, the ceremony came to be customarily performed.

"The Mountain Spirits and the Old Woman,"
a myth of the Chiricahua Indians[175]

Alas, that I should die,
That I should die now,
I who know so much!

It will miss me,
The twirling fire stick;
The fire coal between the hearth stones,
It will miss me.

The Medicine songs,
The songs of magic healing;
The medicine herbs by the water borders,

They will miss me;
The basket willow,
It will miss me;
All the wisdom of women,
It will miss me.

Alas, that I should die,
Who know so much.

The song of a woman abandoned by the tribe
because she is too old to keep up with their
migration, from the southern Shoshone Indians[176]

Once a woman had twin children who fainted
away. Possibly they only slept. Their mother left them
in the morning; and when she returned in the evening,
they were still lying there. She noticed their tracks
around the house: therefore she thought they must
come to life and play during her absence. One day
she stole on them unseen and found them arguing
with each other inside the lodge. One said, "It is
much better to be dead." And the other said, "It is
better to be alive." When they saw her, they stopped
talking, and since then people die from time to time.
There are always some being born and some dying at
the same time, always some living ones and some
dead ones. Had she remained hidden and allowed
them to finish their argument, one would have
prevailed over the other, and there would have been
either no life or no death.

"The Origin of Death," a folk tale of the
Salishan and Sahaptin tribes of the American Indians[177]

It was not until one morning when I found the kitchen unwarmed and the blue enamel saucepan hanging on the wall, that I felt my mother's end to be near. Her illness knew many respites, during which the fire flared up again on the hearth, and the smell of fresh bread and melting chocolate stole under the door together with the cat's impatient paw. These respites were periods of unexpected alarms. My mother and the big walnut cupboard were discovered together in a heap at the foot of the stairs, she having determined to transport it in secret from the upper landing to the ground floor. Whereupon my elder brother insisted that my mother should keep still and that an old servant should sleep in the little house. But how could an old servant prevail against a vital energy so youthful and mischievous that it contrived to tempt and lead astray a body already half fettered by death? My brother, returning before sunrise from attending a distant patient, one day caught my mother red-handed in the most wanton of crimes. Dressed in her nightgown, but wearing heavy gardening sabots, her little gray septuagenarian's plait of hair turning up like a scorpion's tail on the nape of her neck, one foot firmly planted on the cross-piece of the beech trestle, her back bent in the attitude of the expert jobber, my mother, rejuvenated by an indescribable expression of guilty enjoyment, in defiance of all her promises and of the freezing morning dew, was sawing logs in her own yard.

Colette's reminiscences of her mother[178]

The bright sunbeams
Shoot down upon
Tauwara, whose
Lofty ridge veils
Thee from
My sight. O Amo, my beloved,
Leave me, that my eyes
May grieve, and that
They may unceasingly mourn;
For soon must I descend
To the dark shore—
To my beloved who has gone before.

The lament of the dying mother
of a Maori chief[179]

"The other day I thought I was going to say
good-bye to this world. I was hanging up some clothes
to dry. I love to do that, then stand back and watch
and listen to the wind go through the socks or the
pants or the dress, and see the sun warm them and
make them smell fresh. I had dropped a few clothes-
pins, and was picking them up, when suddenly I
could not catch my breath, and a sharp pain seized me
over my chest. I tried hard to stand up, but I couldn't.
I wanted to scream but I knew there was no one
nearby to hear me. My husband had gone to the
store. I sat down on the ground and waited. It was
strong, the pain; and there was no one to tell about
it. I felt as if someone had lassoed me and was pulling
the rope tighter and tighter. Well here you are, an old
cow, being taken in by the good Lord; that is what I
thought.

"I looked at myself, sitting on the ground. For a

second I was my old self again—worrying about how I must have appeared there, worrying about my dress, how dirty it would get to be. This is no place for an old lady, I thought—only for one of my little grandchildren, who love to play out here, build their castles of dirt, wetted down with water I give to them. Then more pain; I thought I had about a minute of life left. I said my prayers. I said goodbye to the house. I pictured my husband in my mind: fifty-seven years of marriage. Such a good man! I said to myself that I might not see him ever again; surely God would take him into Heaven, but as for me, I have no right to expect that outcome. Then I looked up to the sky and waited.

"My eye caught sight of a cloud. It was darker than the rest. It was alone. It was coming my way. The hand of God, I was sure of it! So that is how one dies. All my life, in the spare moments a person has, I wondered how I would go. Now I knew. Now I was ready. I thought I would soon be taken up to the cloud and across the sky I would go, and that would be that. But the cloud kept moving, and soon it was no longer above me, but beyond me; and I was still on my own land, so dear to me, so familiar after all these years. I can't be dead, I thought to myself, if I am here and the cloud is way over there, and getting further each second. Maybe the next cloud—but by then I had decided God had other things to do. Perhaps my name had come up, but He had decided to call others before me and get around to me later. Who can ever know His reasons? Then I spotted my neighbor walking down the road, and I said to myself that I would shout for him. I did, and he heard. But you know, by the time he came I had sprung myself free. Yes, that is right, the pain was all gone."

The words of an old woman of New Mexico[180]

NOTES

INTRODUCTION

* *The Sun Dances, Prayers and Blessings from the Gaelic*, Alexander Carmichael, Christian Community Press, London, 1960, pp. 21 – 23 (invocation of blessing for a young girl, probably on her marriage).

CHAPTER 1:
GIRL-CHILD: THE CELEBRATION OF YOUTH

1. *Breaking Open*, Muriel Rukeyser, Random House, New York, 1973, p. 102 (Eskimo song translated by Paul Radin and Muriel Rukeyser).

2. "To the Anxious Mother," Valente Malangatana, translated by Dorothy Guedes and Philippa Rumsey, in *Poems from Black Africa*, edited by Langston Hughes, Indiana University Press, Bloomington, 1963, p. 128.

3. *Religion of the Kwakiutl Indians*, Franz Boas, Columbia University Press, New York, 1930, p. 283.

4. *Klee Wyck*, Emily Carr, Farrar and Rinehart Inc., New York and Toronto, 1942, p. 39.

5. *Religion of the Kwakiutl Indians*, Franz Boas, Columbia University Press, New York, 1930, p. 284.

6. *Earthly Paradise: An Autobiography*, Colette, edited by Robert Phelps, Farrar, Straus and Giroux, New York, 1966, p. 7.

7. *The Collected Poems of Anne Wilkinson*, edited by A. J. M. Smith, MacMillan Company of Canada Ltd., 1968, pp. 91 – 92.

8. *Lysistrata*, Aristophanes, English version by Dudley

Fitts, Harcourt Brace, New York, 1954, p. 117, lines 1303—1320.

9. *Eskimo Poems from Canada and Greenland,* translated by Tom Lowenstein from material collected by Knud Rasmussen, University of Pittsburgh Press, 1973, pp. 29-30.

10. *An Apache Lifeway: The Economic, Social and Religious Institutions of the Chiricahua Indians,* Morris E. Opler, University of Chicago Press, 1941, reprinted by Cooper Square Publishers, New York, 1965, p. 85.

11. By an anonymous poet in *Ancient Poetry from China, Japan and India,* translated by Henry W. Wells, University of South Carolina Press, Columbia, 1968, p. 265.

CHAPTER 2:
MENSTRUATION: THE PASSAGE
TO MATURITY

12. *Kinaalda—A Study of the Navaho Girls' Puberty Ceremony,* Charlotte Johnson Frisbie, Wesleyan University Press, Middletown, CT, 1967, pp. 296—297.

13. *An Apache Lifeway, op. cit.,* p. 117.

14. *The Sacred Pipe: Black Elk's Account of the Seven Rites of the Ogalala Sioux,* recorded and edited by Joseph Epes Brown, Penguin Books, New York, 1971, pp. 120—121.

15. *American Indian Prose and Poetry—An Anthology,* edited by Margot Astrov, Capricorn Books, New York, 1962, pp. 206—207.

16 . *Navaho Texts,* edited by Harry Hoijer, Linguistic Society of America, Iowa City, 1942, p. 285.

17. *Spider Woman: A Story of Navajo Weavers and Chanters,* Gladys A. Reichard, Macmillan Company, New York, 1934, p. 206.

18. *Fortieth Annual Report of the Bureau of American Ethnology, 1918–19*, pp. 303–304.

19. *Sappho—A New Translation*, Mary Barnard, University of California Press, Berkeley, 1958, p. 25.

20. *The White Pony*, edited by Robert Payne, John Day Company, New York, 1947, p. 49.

21. *Goddesses, Whores, Wives and Slaves: Women in Classical Antiquity*, Sarah B. Pomeroy, Schocken Books, New York, 1975, pp. 137–138.

22. *Marriage in a Matrilineal African Tribe*, Maija Tuupainen, Transactions of the Westermarck Society, vol. xviii, Aurasen Kirjapaino, Forassa, 1970, pp. 149–150.

23. *Alcheringa/Ethnopoetics Two*, vol. 1, 1976, pp. 102–103 (Tristan Tzara poem, translated by Pierre Joris).

24. *Chisungu: A Girl's Initiation Ceremony Among the Bemba of Northern Rhodesia*, Audrey I. Richards, Faber and Faber, London, 1956, p. 205–206.

25. *Folksongs of the Maikal Hills*, Verrier Elwin and Shamrao Hivale, Humphrey Milford and Oxford University Press, London, 1944, p. 20.

CHAPTER 3:
SEPARATION FROM HOME:
THE WEDDING

26. *Songs of Ukrainia with Ruthenian Poems*, translated by Florence Randal Livesay, J. M. Dent and Sons, New York, 1916, pp. 32–33.

27. *Sappho—A New Translation*, op. cit., p. 32.

28. *The Polynesian Family System in Ka'u, Hawaii*, E. S. Craighill Handy and Mary Kawena Pukui, Charles E.

Tuttle and Co., Rutland, VT, new edition, 1972, p. 111–112.

29. *Folklore,* vol. 1, no. 27, p. 431.

30. *Poems by Emily Dickinson,* edited by Martha Dickinson Bianchi and Alfred Leete Hampson, Little, Brown and Company, Boston, 1950, pp. 135–136.

31. *The Poems of Sappho,* by C. H. Haines, George Routledge and Sons, Ltd., New York, 1927, p. 160.

32.*Sappho—A New Translation, op. cit.,* p. 34.

33. *Sappho—One Hundred Lyrics,* Bliss Carman, published for the Florence Press by Chatto and Windus, London, 1910, p. 15.

34. *Songs of Ukrainia with Ruthenian Poems, op. cit.,* pp. 33–35.

35. *Folksongs of the Maikal Hills, op. cit.,* p. 128.

36. *Ibid.,* p. 185.

CHAPTER 4: MARRIED LIFE

37. *Aging: An Album of People Growing Old,* Shura Saul, John Wiley and Sons, Inc., New York, 1972, p. 79.

38. *Christine de Pisan's Ballades, Rondeaux, Virelais—An Anthology,* edited by Kenneth Varty, Leicester University Press, Leicester, England, 1965, translated by C. Meredith Jones, "In praise of marriage," p. 3.

39. *The Orchid Boat: Women Poets of China,* translated and edited by Kenneth Rexroth and Ling Chung, McGraw-Hill, New York, 1972, p. 53.

40. *Cathay,* translations by Ezra Pound, Elkin Matthews, London, 1915, p. 11.

41. *Love and the Turning Year: One Hundred More Poems from the Chinese,* Kenneth Rexroth, New Directions Books, New York, 1970, p. 82.

42. *The Orchid Boat, op. cit.*, p. 67.

43. *Ibid.*, p. 2.

44. *Sappho—A New Translation, op. cit.*, p. 31.

45. *Folksongs of the Maikal Hills, op. cit.*, p. 38.

46. *Ancient Poetry from China, Japan and India, op. cit.*, pp. 47—48.

47. *Folksongs of the Maikal Hills, op. cit.*, p. 34.

48. *Ibid.*, p. 42.

49. *Ibid.*, p. 244.

50. *Ibid.*, p. 98.

51. *Ibid.*, p. 41.

52. *Funk and Wagnall's Dictionary of Folklore, Mythology and Legend*, edited by Maria Leach, Funk and Wagnall's, New York, 1949, p. 1069.

53. *The World Split Open*, edited by Louise Bernikow, Random House, New York, 1974, pp. 192—193.

CHAPTER 5: PASSIONATE WOMAN

54. *The Portable Dorothy Parker*, Brendan Gill, Penguin Books, Baltimore, MD, 1944, p. 303.

55. *Poems by Emily Dickinson, op. cit.*, p. 141.

56. *Folksongs of the Maikal Hills, op. cit.*, pp. 115—116.

57. *The Orchid Boat, op. cit.*, p. 60.

58. *Folksongs of the Maikal Hills, op. cit.*, p. 127.

59. *Ibid.*, p. 124.

60. Daniela Gioseffi in *MS*, vol. 14, no. 7, January 1976, excerpts from pp. 68—69. Also published in *The Great American Belly Dance*, Daniela Gioseffi, Doubleday & Co., New York, 1977.

61. *Technicians of the Sacred: A Range of Poetries from Africa, America, Asia and Oceania*, Jerome Rothenberg, Anchor Books, Doubleday, New York, 1968, pp. 151–152, from a free working by Ed Sanders, published in *Fuck You: Magazine of the Arts*, vol. 5, no. 5, 1963.

62. *The Orchid Boat, op. cit.*, p. 9 (excerpt from "Five Tzu Yeh Songs").

63. *Three Thousand Years of Black Poetry*, edited by Alan Lomax and Raoul Abdul, Dodd, Mead and Company, New York, 1970, p. 30, translated by J. E. Manchip White.

64. *Songs of the Dream People*, edited and translated by J. A. Houston, Longman Canada Ltd., Toronto, 1972, p. 82.

65. *The Orchid Boat, op. cit.*, p. 61.

66. *Folksongs of the Maikal Hills, op. cit.*, p. 239.

67. *The Orchid Boat, op. cit.*, p. 60.

68. "One Way Conversation," in *Ice Age*, Dorothy Livesay, Press Porcepic Ltd., Erin, Ontario, 1975, p. 46.

69. *Alcheringa/Ethnopoetics Two*, vol. 1, 1976, p. 90.

70. *Songs of the Dream People, op. cit.*, p. 8.

71. *The Orchid Boat, op. cit.*, p. 66.

72. *Eskimo Poems from Canada and Greenland, op. cit.*, p. 7.

73. *The Orchid Boat, op. cit.*, p. 11.

74. *Ibid.*, p. 73.

75. *Eskimo Poems from Canada and Greenland, op. cit.*, p. 53.

76. *Poetry of the Negro 1947–1970*, edited by Langston Hughes and Arna Bontemps, Doubleday and Company, New York, 1970.

77. *Goddesses, Whores, Wives and Slaves, op. cit.*, p. 173.

78. *Journal of American Folklore, vol. XVI, no. LXII,* 1903, p. 209.

79. *Poems by Indian Women,* edited by Margaret Macnicol, Calcutta Association Press, Oxford University Press, London, New York, 1923, p. 85 (by Priyambada Debi, born 1872).

80. *African Poems and Love Songs,* Charlotte and Wolf Leslau, Peter Pauper Press, Mount Vernon, NY, 1970, p. 58.

81. *Essays of An Americanist,* Daniel G. Brinton, David McKay, Philadelphia, 1890, p. 295 (Aztec love song).

82. *Shaking the Pumpkin: Traditional Poetry of the Indian North Americas,* Jerome Rothenberg, Doubleday and Company, Garden City, NY, 1972, p. 166, translated by Carl Cary.

83. *Poems by Indian Women, op. cit.,* pp. 65–66 (by Mira Bai, a medieval Indian poet).

CHAPTER 6:
WOMAN'S BODY: THE SEXUAL CENTER

84. *Shaking the Pumpkin, op. cit.,* pp. 282–283, English version by Edward Kissam.

85. "Igbo Poetic Images of Childbirth," in *Folklore,* vol. 84, 1973, p. 142.

86. *Folksongs of the Maikal Hills, op. cit.,* p. 17.

87. *Poems of the Western Highlanders,* G. R. D. McLean, S.P.C.K., London, 1961, p. 275.

88. *By a Woman Writt: Literature from Six Centuries By and About Women,* edited by Joan Goulianos, Penguin Books, Baltimore, MD, 1974, p. 329.

89. *Primitive Song,* C. M. Bowra, Weidenfeld and Nicolson, London, 1962, p. 185.

90. *Sumerian Mythology: A Study of Spiritual and Literary Achievement in the Third Millenium B.C.*, Samuel Noah Kramer, Harper & Brothers, New York, 1961, p. 71.

91. *Nectar in a Sieve*, Kamala Markandaya, Putnam's, London, 1954, excerpts from pp. 70—72.

92. *Technicians of the Sacred: A Range of Poetries from Africa, America, Asia and Oceania*, edited by Jerome Rothenberg, Doubleday and Company, NY, 1969, p. 101, originally published by W. G. Archer, "The Illegitimate Child in Santal Society," *Man in India XXIV*, 1944, 156—58.

93. *Earthly Paradise: An Autobiography, op. cit.*, pp. 199—200.

94. *Travelling Standing Still*, Genevieve Taggard, Alfred A. Knopf, New York, 1928, p. 35.

95. *Folksongs of the Maikal Hills, op. cit.*, p. 246.

96. *The World Split Open*, edited by Louise Bernikow, Random House, New York, 1974, p. 151, Sylvia Pankhurst in *Writ on Cold Slate* (1922).

97. *A Bird in the House*, Margaret Laurence, McClelland and Stewart Ltd., Toronto, 1970, pp. 22—23.

98. *Folksongs of the Maikal Hills, op. cit.*, p. 236 (pregnancy song).

99. *Waterlily Fire Poems 1935—1962*, Muriel Rukeyser, Macmillan, New York, 1962, p. 139, stanza V, p. 140, stanza VIII (excerpts from "Nine Poems for the Unborn Child").

100. *Shaking the Pumpkin, op. cit.*, p. 50, English version by Anselm Hollo.

101. *Four Masterpieces of American Indian Literature*, edited and translated by John Bierhorst, Farrar, Straus and Giroux, New York, 1974, pp. 158, 159 (The Twelfth Article of the Ritual of Condolence).

102. *The Kalevala: or, Poems of the Kaleva District*, Elias Lönnrot, comp., Francis P. Magoun, Jr., tr., Harvard University Press, Cambridge, MA, 1963, pp. 334–335.

103. *Blessing Way*, Leland C. Wyman, translated by Fr. Bernard Haile, O.F.M., University of Arizona Press, Tucson, 1970, pp. 336-337.

104. *The Sun Dances, op. cit.*, p. 114 (Bride was thought to aid at the birth of Jesus).

105. *The Great Mother*, Erich Neumann, Princeton University Press, 1955, pp. 135–136.

106. *Lunar Baedeker and Timetables: Selected Poems*, Mina Loy, Jonathan Williams, Highlands, NC, 1958, pp. 45–49.

107. *The Old Kalevala and Certain Antecedents*, Elias Lönnrot, comp., Francis P. Magoun, Jr., tr., Harvard University Press, Cambridge, MA, 1969, Poem 25, lines 61–106.

108. "Birthsongs of the Macha Galla," Lambert Bartels, in *Ethnology*, vol. 8, 1969, p. 415.

109. *Lunar Baedeker and Timetables, op. cit.*, pp. 48–49.

110. "Igbo Poetic Images of Childbirth," op. cit., pp. 144–145.

111. *Under a Glass Bell and Other Stories*, Anais Nin, E. P. Dutton, New York, 1948, pp. 100–101.

112. *Collected Poems*, Alice Meynell, Burns and Oates, London, 1913, p. 107.

113. *The American Rhythm*, Mary Austin, Houghton Mifflin Company, Boston, 1930. (Mary Austin (1868–1934) was an early interpreter of American Indian tribal songs.)

114. "Birthsongs of the Macha Galla," op. cit., p. 414.

115. *Annie Allen*, Gwendolyn Brooks, Harper & Brothers, New York, 1949, p. 3.

116. *My Life*, Isadora Duncan, Liveright Press, New York, 1955, p. 196.

117. *African Poems and Love Songs, op. cit.*, p. 16.

118. *Kingship and the Gods: A Study of Ancient Near Eastern Religion as the Integration of Society and Nature*, Henri Frankfort, University of Chicago Press, 1948, p. 174.

119. *Waterlily Fire Poems 1935—1962, op. cit.*, p. 158.

120. *Primitive Song, op. cit.*, p. 177.

121. *Earthly Paradise: An Autobiography, op. cit.*, pp. 203—204.

122. *Breaking Open, op. cit.*, pp. 100—101. Eskimo song translated by Paul Radin and Muriel Rukeyser).

123. *By a Woman Writt, op. cit.*, p. 45.

124. *Ibid.*, pp. 328—329.

CHAPTER 7: MOTHERHOOD

125. *Sappho—A New Translation, op. cit.*, p. 17.

126. *By a Woman Writt, op. cit.*, p. 154.

127. *The Collected Poems of Anne Wilkinson, op. cit.*, p. 94.

128. *Five Short Novels*, Doris Lessing, St. Albans, Hertfordshire, England, Granada Publishing Co., 1953, p. 255.

129. *Folksongs of the Maikal Hills, op. cit.*, p. 256.

130. *Klee Wyck, op. cit.*, pp. 36—37.

131. *The Sun Dances, op. cit.*, pp. 70—71.

132. *African Poems and Love Songs, op. cit.*, p. 23.

133. *Good News About the Earth*, Lucille Clifton, Random House, New York, 1972, p. 4.

134. *Selected Poems*, Gwendolyn Brooks, Harper & Row, New York, 1963, p. 4, © *1945*

135. *Ice Age, op. cit.*, p. 28.

136. *Letters Home*, Sylvia Plath, selected and edited by Aurelia Schober Plath, Harper & Row, New York, 1975, p. 450.

137. *Religion of the Kwakiutl Indians, op. cit.*, p. 202.

138. *The Oxford Book of Greek Verse in Translation*, edited by T. F. Higham and C. M. Bowra, Clarendon Press, Oxford, 1938, p. 667, no. 674, translated by A. J. Butler.

139. *Journal of American Folklore*, vol. XVI, no. LXIII, 1903, p. 208.

140. *Primitive Song, op. cit.*, p. 198 (from the Dama tribe of North Africa).

141. *Sunflower Splendour: Three Thousand Years of Chinese Poetry*, coedited by Wu-chi Liu and Irving Yu cheng Lo, Indiana University Press, Bloomington, 1976, pp. 38−39, lines 61−102 of "The Lamentation," by Ts'ai Yen, A.D. 200.

142. *Stone and Flower Poems 1935-43*, Kathleen Raine, Nicolson and Watson, London, 1943, p. 13.

143. *Alcheringa/Ethnopoetics Two*, vol. 1, 1976, p. 88 (mourning song from Ghana).

144. *Seeds as They Fall*, Helen Sorrells, Vanderbilt University Press, Nashville, TN, 1971, first published in *Shenandoah*, © 1966.

145. *Eskimo Poems from Canada and Greenland, op. cit., pp. 41−42.*

146. *Canadian Poetry: The Modern Era*, edited by John Newlove, McClelland and Stewart Ltd., Toronto, 1977, p. 87, originally published in *Within the Zodiac*, Phyllis Gotlieb, McClelland, Stewart Ltd., Toronto, 1964.

CHAPTER 8: THE CHANGING SEASONS

147. *Poems Selected and New 1950-1974*, Adrienne Rich, W. W. Norton and Co., New York, 1975, p. 61.

148. *Ibid.*, pp. 109—110.

149. *Snapshots of a Daughter-in-Law Poems 1954—1962*, Adrienne Rich, W. W. Norton and Co., New York, 1967, p. 35.

150. *My Lady of the Chinese Courtyard*, Elizabeth Cooper, Peter Davies Ltd., London, 1920.

151. *Folksongs of the Maikal Hills, op. cit.*, p. 276.

152. Charlotte Brontë in *The Women Poets in English*, edited by Ann Stanford, McGraw-Hill and Co., New York, 1972, p. 121.

153. *Collected Poems: Two Seasons*, Dorothy Livesay, McGraw-Hill Ryerson Ltd., Canada, 2nd ed., 1972, p. 239.

154. *No Voyage and Other Poems*, Mary Oliver, Houghton Mifflin Company, Boston, 1965.

155. *Ice Age, op. cit.*, p. 33.

156. *The Old Ones of New Mexico*, Robert Coles, University of New Mexico Press, Albuquerque, 1949, p. 59.

157. *Ancient Poetry from China, Japan and India, op. cit.*, p. 45.

158. *Collected Poems: Two Seasons, op. cit.*, p. 241.

159. *The Oxford Book of Greek Verse in Translation, op. cit.*, p. 60.

160. *Alcheringa/Ethnopoetics Two*, vol. 1, 1976, p. 82 ("Mourning Song of the Ba-Totela," by Tristan Tzara).

161. *American Indian Prose and Poetry, op. cit.*, p. 101, from *The Osage Tribe* by Francis La Flesche (d. 1932) (the weaver's lamentation from the shrine ritual).

162. *Knowing Woman*, Irene Claremont de Castillejo, G. P. Putnam for the C. J. Jung Foundation for Analyti-

cal Psychology, New York, 1973, p. 156.

163. *Earthly Paradise: An Autobiography, op. cit.*, pp. 58–59.

164. *An Apache Lifeway, op. cit.*, p. 128.

165. *Breaking Open, op. cit.*, p. 18.

166. *Folksongs of the Maikal Hills, op. cit.*, p. 257.

167. *By a Woman Writt, op. cit.*, pp. 79–80.

168. *Ice Age, op. cit.*, p. 68.

169. *Eskimo Poems from Canada and Greenland, op. cit.*, p. 33.

170. *Ice Age, op. cit.*, p. 27.

171. *Shaking the Pumpkin, op. cit.*, 159, English version by Armand Schwerner from *Poemes Eskimo*, Paul Emile Victor, Pierre Seghers, Paris, 1958.

172. *Folksongs of the Maikal Hills, op. cit.*, p. 248.

173. *Working*, Studs Terkel, Avon Press, New York, 1972, p. 626 (from Ruth Lindstrom's Recollections).

174. *Complete Poems of Emily Jane Brontë*, edited by C. W. Halfield, Columbia University Press, New York, 1941, p. 142.

175. *American Indian Prose and Poetry, op. cit.*, p. 211.

176. *The Women Poets in Engish, op. cit.*, pp. 165–166 (southern Sohone song, reworking by Mary Austin, originally published in *The American Rhythm*, Mary Austin, Houghton Mifflin, Boston, 1930.

177. *Folktales of Salishan and Sahaptin Tribes*, edited by Franz Boas, American Folklore Society, Lancaster, PA, and New York, 1917, p. 125.

178. *Earthly Paradise: An Autobiography, op. cit.*, p. 22.

179. "Primitive Woman as Poet," *Journal of American Folklore*, vol. XVI, no. LXIII, 1903, p. 209.

180. *The Old Ones of New Mexico, op. cit.*, pp. 7–8.